THE LOST ART OF DISCIPLE MAKING

THE LOST ART OF DISCIPLE MAKING

LEROY EIMS

Foreword by Robert E. Coleman

 ZONDERVAN PUBLISHING HOUSE
OF THE ZONDERVAN CORPORATION
GRAND RAPIDS. MICHIGAN 49506

NAVPRESS
A MINISTRY OF THE NAVIGATORS
Colorado Springs. Colorado 80901

Library of Congress Cataloging in Publication Data

Eims, LeRoy.
    The lost art of disciple making.

    Bibliography: p.
    1. Christian life—1960-   2. Christian
leadership.   I.   Title.
BV4501.2.E32   248'.4   78-17227
ISBN 0-310-37281-X

To

Dr. Clyde W. Taylor

a man mightily used of God around the globe
in seeing spiritually qualified laborers
raised up to the glory of God

CONTENTS

FOREWORD

Jesus came to save the world, and to that end He died, but on His way to the cross He concentrated His life on making a few disciples. These men were taught to do the same, until through the process of reproduction, the gospel of the kingdom would reach to the ends of the earth.

The way God's Son lived thus became a pattern to all who follow in His steps—a principle explicated clearly in the command to "make disciples of all nations." How they are made, of course, will be conditioned on particular gifts and roles in society, but everyone who believes on Christ is called to His work within their own vocation and life style.

Unfortunately, few Christians seem to understand what this means, at least when it comes to daily living. Even persons who are in leadership positions of the church often have no idea how to go about teaching others to observe all things that Jesus commanded. Where this pertains it is not surprising that believers fail to go very far in their pilgrimage of faith, much less develop the potential of their ministry.

That is why this volume is such a pleasure to commend. It comes to grips with the real work of discipling men, not in vague institutional programs, but in clear guidelines for personal initiative. The treatment is simple and to the point. Our Lord's mandate need not be a lost art to those who will take to heart the counsel found in these pages.

Giving authenticity to the book, while enhancing its down-to-earth appeal, is the author's own experience. LeRoy

Eims writes as a practitioner, not a theoretician. For years he has been actively involved in shaping the lives of men. There are scores of persons today in harvest fields around the world who bear witness to his faithful labors with them.

His approach reflects the strategy of The Navigators where he serves as International Ministry Representative. But what he says is not the property of any organization. This is basic New Testament discipleship. Anyone can profit from its reading. Best of all, the application of its truth can bring new meaning and excitement into living—living in the fulfillment of the great commission.

—ROBERT E. COLEMAN
Asbury Theological Seminary

PREFACE

When my daughter Becky was in grade school, we often took walks together. We would stroll among the towering pine trees, the scrub oak, and various plants and flowers in a beautiful area near our home. One day we had a conversation about a scrawny little bush that was growing along our path. I explained to Becky that we should be proud of that little bush, because even though it wasn't nearly as big as the magnificent blue spruce growing nearby, it had grown to its maximum potential. It was as fully developed as it could be with the amount of rain and sunshine it had obtained. It had not held back; it had grown to its limit.

Babies are somewhat like that too. They will grow if someone will help a little. They are only too happy to eat if someone will but put milk in the bottle or take the cap off the jar of strained peas and spoon them in.

Now that Becky has grown up, married, and had a child of her own, I watch with amazement as she feeds her daughter. When little Joy Elise sees the food, it prompts all the excitement of a circus coming to town. All we have to do is get the food within her reach and Joy will do the rest.

Every believer in Jesus Christ deserves the opportunity of personal nurture and development. Every new believer is expected to achieve his or her full potential for God. And most of them *would* if they had the opportunity, if someone would get the food within reach, if someone would give them the help they need, if someone would give them the training they

11

should have, and if someone would care enough to suffer a little, sacrifice a little, and pray a lot.

In this book we want to look at the growth process in the life of a Christian, from the time that person comes to Christ to his or her becoming a disciple and then a worker for Him. We will examine what nurture and guidance it takes to develop spiritually qualified workers in the church of Jesus Christ.

The concepts and principles we will be suggesting and examining do not emerge from a philosophy of speedy growth and instant maturity. True growth takes time and tears and love and patience. On the leader's part, it takes the faith to see people as God expects them to be and wants them to become. And it takes some knowledge to help get them there.

This book does not pretend to be the entire chain in the training process; it does not presume to contain all the answers to the problems of spiritual growth. In fact, it does not even presume to have many answers to many problems. What it does try to do is provide some information to help Christian leaders strengthen one small link in the entire chain of their ministry for Christ. It is not the whole chain. It deals only with one link: how to train spiritually qualified workers for Christ.

The book is based on a study of the Word of God and the experience of many in an organization committed to making disciples and helping produce workers for the cause of Christ. It is sent out with the prayer that the Holy Spirit will use it to strengthen a weak link here and there, thus helping Christians to be better equipped and more effective in their service for the Lord.

LeRoy Eims
Colorado Springs, Colorado
January 1978

ACKNOWLEDGMENT

I spent the spring and summer of 1973 with Marvin Smith, who is now director of The Navigators ministry in Africa, while he and his family were home on furlough. We had many hours of fellowship together discussing the basic approach to the ministry of developing spiritually qualified workers.

Marvin had spent many months analyzing the overall concepts, while I had struggled for about half a year thinking through the step-by-step details and specifics of making disciples. Both of us had been practicing these things for many years, but had never codified them in our thinking.

As we talked, we discovered that our research meshed into one solid whole. We could now write out and clearly communicate to others what we had been doing with the biblical principles we had learned over the years.

Much of what this book contains, including the chart in Appendix 2, emerged from the study Marvin and I did together.

THE
LOST
ART
OF
DISCIPLE
MAKING

CHAPTER 1

THE NEED FOR MULTIPLYING DISCIPLES

"And the word of God increased; and the number of the disciples multiplied in Jerusalem greatly" (Acts 6:7, KJV).

One day I received a phone call from a busy pastor. Could we get together, he asked, some place, sometime to talk about training people in his church? He was willing to fly anywhere in the United States to meet me and discuss his problem for half a day or so. He obviously needed help, so we set up a meeting.

As we spent some time together, I found his situation to be fairly typical. He was the pastor of a growing, healthy, and flourishing church. People were coming to Christ, attendance had increased, and he had to have two morning worship services. God was clearly blessing in many wonderful ways.

But he also had a problem. He knew that unless he trained some spiritually qualified workers among the men and women of his congregation, many people would not get needed help in the initial stages of Christian growth (adequate follow-up) and would not develop into strong, robust disciples of Jesus Christ. And the pastor knew he was the key to this. The whole process had to begin with him. He could not toss it to a "department," nor delegate it to someone else. As the spiritual leader of these people, he had to lead the way.

He had another problem—he was already a busy man. Many things demanded his attention; many people demanded his time. Like many pastors, he spent a good deal of his time putting out brush fires in his congregation. No sooner had he dealt with one problem than another one arose.

To his consternation and frustration, he spent too much time with problem-centered people, trying to settle quarrels, make peace between members, deal with difficult family situations, and a 101 other things.

But he had a dream. At times, he would go into his study, lock the door, and think of his situation in a whole new light. *Wouldn't it be great,* he would think to himself, *if I had a dedicated, ever-growing band of spiritually qualified men and women who could help handle some of the "spiritual" problems that keep coming up in this church?*

He did not mean people who merely took tapes of his sermons to the shut-ins, delivered food, clothing, and financial aid to the needy, taught in the Sunday school, or helped him manage the business and financial affairs of the church. He meant people who knew how to win another person to Christ and then take that person from the time of his conversion and help him become a solid, dedicated, committed, fruitful, mature disciple who could in time repeat that process in the life of another.

He would smile there in the privacy of his study, for his dream was so vivid he could almost reach out and touch that which he envisioned. But then he would be jarred back to reality by the ringing of the phone. Another problem. And he was the only spiritually qualified person in the congregation who could help. So he would set aside his dream, pick up his Bible, and go out the door.

Disciples in Action

Let's look at another scene. Four couples are meeting for a Bible study on a weeknight. They have been getting together for about four months, since three of them had been converted to Christ. One of the laymen in the church has been leading the study, and they have just settled down for one of their lively discussions. As they launch into their lesson, the phone rings.

"Is Joe there?" Joe is one of the four-month-old Christians.

"Yes, but he's busy right now. He's in a Bible study."

The voice is desperate, "Please! I've got to talk with him."

"OK."

Joe picks up the phone and listens. "OK," he says, "I'll come right over."

Joe comes back to his Bible study group and explains. His business partner wants him to come over and help him. There's been a marital fight, and the man's wife is walking out on him. The whole mess has been brewing for a long time, and Joe feels he should go and do what he can.

The leader of the study group says he thinks it's the right thing to do, and while Joe's gone the group will pray. So Joe, a four-month-old Christian, picks up his Bible and goes out the door to try to save a marriage. The Bible study turns into a prayer meeting.

That scene is a real situation with real people. The leader of that group told me about it a few days after it happened. At the time he hadn't heard from Joe on how his meeting with his partner had gone. I saw that leader again about three weeks later and heard the great news. Joe had been used of God to lead both husband and wife to Christ. He was now in the process of leading them in a study of the Scriptures.

The leader, in turn, had begun to spend a little extra time with Joe to answer some of his questions now that he and his wife were leading new Christians in a study of the Word of God. Though Joe had always been eager, he was more so now. He needed a great deal of help and knew it. The leader was only too glad to do what he could. He could see that the Lord was using that time to deepen their relationship and to deepen Joe's life in the Lord.

It was also a challenge to the other couples in Joe's study group. It had become evident to them that sooner or later the Lord would give them an opportunity to share with others some of the things they were learning. It made the study that much more meaningful to all of them.

That scene, with variations, is being repeated in many places around the world. It is not an isolated incident. In fact, the story of the pastor who met with me, mentioned earlier in this chapter, has a happy ending. After we'd spent the day together discussing making disciples and training workers, he went back to his church and began putting into practice the principles which I shared with him and which are taught in this book.

Today, there is a steady stream of disciples and workers who emerge from his ministry to affect their neighborhoods and friends for Christ. These people from his church are being used of God to win others to Christ and to help their converts, in turn, repeat the process.

This concept of multiplying disciples has not always been as widely accepted as it is today. At one time, in fact, not too long ago, relatively few people were doing it. But many more today are returning to that biblical process.

The Crucial Element of Personal Help

Shortly after my wife, Virginia, and I became Christians, we met Waldron Scott, a young man about our age who took a personal interest in us. He had been helped in his Christian life by a fellow serviceman while he was stationed on Guam with the Air Force in World War II. We were classmates in college, and he came over to our home once a week or so to share spiritual truths with us and to help us in our spiritual growth.

His actual working with us began on the day I asked him why there seemed to be such an obvious difference in our Christian lives, why he was like he was and Virginia and I were like we were. He was able to quote the Scriptures like he knew them by heart; fairly regularly he would share how God had answered his prayers; he seemed to know his Bible well.

He came over that night and asked me some questions. Did I read my Bible regularly? No, hardly ever. Did I study it? Again, no. Did I memorize it? Aha, here I had him. The previous Sunday our pastor had preached on Matthew 6:33, and I had been so impressed by the verse that I memorized it when I got home.

"Great," Scotty said, "Quote it for me. Let's hear it."

I couldn't remember it. I realized then that there was something lacking in my Scripture memory program.

Then he asked, "Do you pray?"

"Well, yes," I told him. "At meal times I repeat a prayer I have memorized." We were just sitting down for some refreshments, so I said my prayer: "Bless the food which now we take, to do us good for Jesus' sake. Amen."

During the course of the evening it became obvious that there was much more to prayer than that. He offered to meet with my wife and me and share some of the things that had been of help to him. We were eager to do so.

We began. Scotty taught us how to read the Bible and get something out of our reading. He taught us how to do personal Bible study and, with the help of the Holy Spirit, apply its lessons to our lives. He taught us to memorize the Word so that it would be available to the Holy Spirit 24 hours a day. He taught us how to assimilate the Scriptures into the spiritual bloodstream of our lives through meditation on the Word. He taught us how to pray and expect answers from God. That was a blessed year for us. We were eager to learn, and Scotty was willing to spend time with us.

The next year I began my sophomore year and Scotty continued to meet with us. We were continuing to grow and my Christian life was full of new discoveries. We had discovered the high adventure of abundant Christian living, as the Lord was becoming more personal and real in our lives.

Midway through the first semester, a classmate came up to me and said, "You know, LeRoy, I've been watching you. Your Christian life is sure on a different plane than mine." And he began asking some questions, essentially what I had asked Scotty the year before.

I smiled and asked, "Well, do you read your Bible regularly?"

"No."

"Do you study it?" No again.

"Do you memorize the Scriptures?" No, he didn't do that either.

"Do you pray?" Still no.

I suggested we get together and talk about these things. He was eager and enthusiastic, so we began. I shared with him the things Scotty had shared with me, and he began to grow in his Christian life. He began to dig into the Word, pray, witness, and the Spirit of God worked mightily in his life that year.

The following year I transferred to the University of Washington, and my friend transferred to another school. A few months after school began I received an interesting letter from him. He had been attending a Christian fellowship on campus and a fellow student had come up to him and asked him about his Christian life. It seemed this student had noticed a difference and wanted to find out about it. So my friend asked him some questions that had to do with Bible reading, study, memory, and prayer. He had shown a keen interest in doing these things, so my friend had begun to share with him on a regular basis the things he had learned from me and which I had learned from Scotty.

Meanwhile, a Christian student had come up to me on the University of Washington campus . . . and so it goes. For many years now I have been involved in helping others personally in their Christian lives. I've watched the interest pastors, missionaries, dedicated laymen, college and seminary students, and servicemen have shown in helping others individually as well. Today a growing groundswell of interest in multiplying disciples is to be seen in many churches and by many people.

To Multiply or Not to Multiply—That Is the Question

Some years ago I was talking to a zealous young Christian. "Bob," I asked, "what's the thing that brings you more joy than anything else in life?"

"Man, LeRoy, that's easy," he replied. "Leading someone to Christ."

I agreed with him. Everybody is happy when that happens—you are happy, the new convert is happy, there is joy in heaven. "But," I told Bob, "there is something even greater than that."

He was puzzled. What could possibly be greater than seeing a person come to Christ?

I continued, "When the person you have led to Christ grows and develops into a dedicated, fruitful, mature disciple who then goes on to lead others to Christ and help them in turn as well."

"Say!" he exclaimed, "I've never thought of that!"

Frankly, it is no surprise that he hadn't heard or thought of that. In those days the idea was pretty obscure, but he was willing to take the time to learn, and he did. Today there are many mature, committed, fruitful disciples on two continents because of the impact of Bob's life and his vision of multiplying disciples.

On the other hand, a lack of knowledge of these things can

have sad consequences. I was visiting a foreign mission field and spoke with a veteran missionary. He told me a story that still haunts me; I can't get it out of my mind. It seems that he went overseas some fifteen years before we met and began the usual programs. About the time he arrived on his field, he met a young man named Johnny, who was involved in something quite different.

Johnny was a committed disciple of Jesus Christ, but he was going about his ministry in all the wrong ways according to the "book." In contrast to the typical missionary approach of the time, Johnny was spending the bulk of his time meeting with a few young men in that country. The veteran missionary tried to get Johnny straightened out, but the young man kept on with his "different" approach. The years passed, and the veteran missionary now had to leave the country of his service due to new visa restrictions.

As he sat across the coffee table from me in his home, he told me, "LeRoy, I've got little to show for my time there. Oh, there is a group of people who meet in our assembly, but I wonder what will happen to them when I leave. They are not disciples. They have been faithful in listening to my sermons, but they do not witness. Few of them know how to lead another person to Christ. They know nothing about discipling others. And now that I am leaving, I can see I've all but wasted my time here."

He continued, "Then I look at what has come out of Johnny's life. One of the men he worked with is now a professor at the university. This man is mightily used of God to reach and train scores of university students. Another is leading a witnessing and discipling team of about forty young men and women. Another is in a nearby city with a group of thirty-five growing disciples around him. Three have gone to other countries as missionaries and are now leading teams in those lands who are multiplying disciples. God is blessing their work.

"I see the contrast between my life and his and it is tragic. I was so sure I was right. What he was doing seemed so insignificant, but now I look at the results and they are staggering." It was a sad meeting for both of us.

On another occasion I was speaking at a weekend conference in the Midwest. A pastor who had spent the bulk of his life as a missionary in the Middle East and was now in a nearby city came to the conference. In the opening meeting, I shared this passage with the conferees: "It was he who gave some to be apostles, some to be prophets, some to be evangelists, and some to be pastors and teachers, to prepare God's people for works of service, so that the body of Christ may be built up" (Eph. 4:11-12).

I tried to explain that the thrust of that passage was that God had given leaders to the church in order to build up and train the rest of us in the work of the ministry. I said that the ministry of the gospel was to be done by all of us—laymen and clergy alike. All of us together are to be a great witnessing brotherhood, but we need training.

After the meeting this man came up to me and held out his Greek New Testament. "That's exactly what it says," he stated.

With that he turned and walked away, went to his room, packed his bags, and started to leave the conference. I was startled by his actions, so I stopped him and asked if we had offended him in some way. Was there anything for which we should apologize and ask his forgiveness?

"Not at all," he replied. "I've got all I need. My people are going to hear about this!" With that he got into his car and drove off. He simply wanted to be back with his people that very Sunday, preach to them that very message, and begin practicing it in his ministry.

In recent years I have watched the country where he had served for so many years blow up with bitter hatreds and racial strive. I've often wondered if it might have been a different story had he gone there thirty years ago with the vision of discipling a band of men and women, something like Johnny had done on another mission field.

One spring, a colleague of mine and I taught a workshop at a seminary in their School of Evangelism. The workshop ran for three days, was about two-and-a-half hours long, and was well attended. Our topic was "Discipleship in the Local Church."

During one of our discussion sessions, an elderly pastor spoke up and told us of his own experience in discipling some of the men in his church. He had started this about three years before and now had a band of stalwart, faithful men on whom he could call at a moment's notice. He had started with one man; later he and this man worked with two others who had expressed interest. The discipling process continued, and after a time the four of them began to meet with four others. The ministry had multiplied till he now had this dedicated band of men who were truly spiritually qualified to work in the ministry of the church.

The elderly pastor told us it was by far the most rewarding, fulfilling, and exciting thing that had happened to him in thirty-five years in the ministry. After this account, the eyes of many of the young seminarians began to gleam with anticipation. They could hardly wait to get out into the pastorate and begin their own ministry of multiplying disciples.

The Indianapolis Model

Dr. Roy Blackwood has been a close personal friend of mine for years. He has been multiplying disciples since he went to Indianapolis, Indiana to form a new congregation in his denomination. He determined to build his ministry on this philosophy of training men to train others in discipleship and in making disciples.

He did not want to be just a Bible teacher to a group of spiritually hungry souls who would get their only ration of spiritual food once a week from his sermons. He wanted to train a band of strong, rugged soldiers of the Cross who would then collaborate with him in the work of the ministry in the church.

Some years have now passed and his ministry has proved to be one of the unique expressions of discipleship in our day. Roy has his disciples. In fact, when he and his wife went around the world on a preaching and lecture tour, he left the church in the able hands of the people whom he had trained and was gone for almost a year.

During his absence, the men preached the sermons and directed the activities of the church. They *did* the ministry and the Lord blessed their efforts as the congregation grew and flourished under their leadership. When Roy and his wife returned from their trip, he wondered if there could still be a place and a need for him. There was, of course, but he would work with the others in the ministry of multiplying disciples.

Some years ago a man came to me with what he thought

was a great idea. He was bubbling over with enthusiasm and was eager to secure my participation in his plan to forward the work of Christ. So I listened carefully. When he had finished, I declined his offer to become involved. He was surprised and asked why I would not work with him.

"Two reasons," I replied. "One, it is not scriptural. Two, it won't work."

What I enjoy so much about the ministry of multiplying disciples is that it is scriptural and it works. It is a scriptural approach to helping fulfill Christ's Great Commission (Matt. 28:18-20), and helping to do something about training workers (Matt. 9:37-38) who today, as in Christ's day, are still few.

Second, I have seen it in action for over twenty-five years and it works. When some of us were involved in a ministry of multiplying disciples in the 1950s, we didn't have it well codified and organized. We just called it "working with a few men (or women)." But since those days I've watched pastors, housewives, missionaries, nurses, building contractors, school teachers, seminary professors, and grocery owners get involved in the lives of a few people. I have seen the Lord bless their efforts and multiply their lives in Christ into the lives of others.

This is not a cure-all, of course, but few things are. But I do know this. When you start spending individual time with another Christian for the purpose of having a ministry in his or her life—time together in the Word, prayer, fellowship, systematic training—something happens in your own life as well. May God grant you patience, love, and perseverance as you begin to share the life He has given you with others.

CHAPTER 2

BIBLICAL EXAMPLES
OF DISCIPLESHIP TRAINING

"When morning came, he called his disciples to him and chose twelve of them, whom he also designated apostles" (Luke 6:13).

When a pastor looks out over his congregation on Sunday morning, what does he see? Many things. He sees some non-Christians perhaps, some seeking, some curious, and some who have been brought to church by concerned friends. He sees people with heavy hearts crushed with sorrow, people on whom the pressures, disappointments, and heartaches of life have fallen.

He sees young Christians, who are eager and thrilled with their new lives in Christ. He sees "old" Christians, who have heard it all before and who respond to the most stirring challenge with a hearty yawn. He sees the faithful, who are there every time the doors open.

He sees the newly married. He sees those whose marriages are in trouble. He sees families with financial problems, hospital bills, and businesses that are not doing well. He sees the successful businessman. He sees the husband who has lost his job and the farmer whose crops must have rain soon or he will lose everything. And so on around the congregation.

As the pastor stands there before his people, a thought crosses his mind, *How can I minister to these people and meet their needs with a message or two a week?* The congregation probably has as many needs as there are people in it. What is the answer to his dilemma?

To answer his question, we must first ask, "Did Jesus ever face anything like that? Did He have crowds before Him with a variety of needs?" The Gospels clearly indicate that He did. His ministry was filled with miracles, multitudes, long hours, weariness, and spiritual conflicts. Lepers came who needed His touch; blind men called His name as He passed by. Lawyers tried to trick Him. Sinners of all kinds and of both sexes loved Him, provided Him with meals, and washed His feet with their tears. Cheering throngs followed Him; crowds later demanded His death. His life was filled with every type of emotion, every type of opposition, every type of activity.

Toward the end of His ministry Jesus spoke with His Father in His great high priestly prayer—interceding for His disciples. In it He made a startling statement, "I have brought you glory on earth by completing the work you gave me to do" (John 17:4).

Why is that so remarkable? Didn't Jesus glorify God with every thought, word, and deed every moment of every day of His life among men? Yes He did, and that is amazing in light of our own failures along these lines. But the truly astounding thing is His statement, "I have finished the work which thou gavest me to do" (KJV).

Most of us are familiar with Christ's work of redemption and remember His words from the cross, "It is finished" (John 19:30). By that final and glorious act, He purchased our redemption; He died for our sins; He set us free.

What then did He mean in His prayer when He said, "I have finished the work"? When you read the prayer carefully, you'll notice that He did not mention miracles or multitudes, but forty times He referred to the men whom God had given Him out of the world. *These men were His work.* His ministry touched thousands, but He trained twelve men. He gave His life on the cross for millions, but during the three and a half years of His ministry He gave His life uniquely to twelve men.

In our teaching and preaching we often clearly emphasize Christ's ministry of redemption, and we certainly should do that. But we also need to study, understand, and proclaim His ministry of training in the lives of these few men. Three principles may be seen in this training.

The Principle of Selection

The men whom Jesus chose were ordinary people—
fishermen, tax collectors, and others like them. When it came
time to choose those whom He would train, He spent the night
in prayer. "One of those days Jesus went out into the hills to
pray, and spent the night praying to God. When morning
came, he called his disciples to him and chose twelve of them,
whom he also designated apostles" (Luke 6:12-13).

This is an important point in selection. He did not hastily
rush out and grab the first people who showed interest. To Him
this was a momentous decision that would have far-reaching
consequences. How far reaching? Humanly speaking, we can't
even guess, but we do know this. The consequences of that
ministry have continued to this day and by the grace of God will
continue through our lives into the lives of thousands in the
years to come.

Whoever is thinking about or is now involved in a ministry
of making disciples (Matt. 28:19) should think soberly about
this matter of selection. It is much easier to ask a man to come
with you than to ask him to leave if you learn, much to your
chagrin and sorrow, that you have chosen the wrong man.

Why did Jesus choose men with very human tendencies
and failings? Suppose He had chosen only those who were
highly cultured, of great intellect and wealth, who never had
any nagging doubts or fears, men who never made mistakes or
said things they later regretted, those who were strangers to
the infirmities, desires, problems, and sins of the rest of us.
Where would that put us? We couldn't identify with people
like that. We would be tempted to throw up our hands in
despair, turn around, and continue in our mediocre ways.

Not only were they common men, they were individuals.
They were not all alike, twelve photocopies of each other. They
were not twelve wooden soldiers carved from the same diagram, twelve cardboard replicas cut from the same pattern,
twelve plastic statues taken from the same mold. For example,
Simon the Zealot hated the Romans who occupied Palestine,
while Matthew the tax collector worked for them.

What does that teach us? What application to our lives can
we draw? One lesson is obvious. In our making disciples, we

should not select only those who are like us in temperament and personality. Nor should we choose only those who act in a certain way that we find agreeable to our personal lives and acceptance standards. It would be a good idea to have some "roughnecks" on the team as well as some scholars and quiet types.

The work of Christ is a many-splendored thing, and there are times when the man who is rough and ready will be more fit for a particular task than the philosophical theorist and vice versa. God loves variety. In nature you'll find the wild rose, the blue spruce, the palm tree, the cactus, the magnolia, and the sunflower. At the zoo you'll marvel at the giraffe, hippo, gazelle, boa constrictor, hummingbird, and eagle. In selecting men and women, you'll have to abandon your proneness to conformity and follow the example of Jesus.

His men were called Galileans; they were people who were considered a bit provincial and old fashioned by their more sophisticated brothers in Jerusalem. They were generally a hard-working lot when compared to the philosophical dreamers and scholars of the big city. They did not already know it all, so they were more teachable than the cultured class whose home was Jerusalem. This is not to say that Jesus shunned men of culture and education. He had a lengthy conversation with Nicodemus, a member of the Jewish ruling council and a teacher in Israel; He did later choose Saul of Tarsus to be one of His leaders in the church.

The Principle of Association

For what purpose did Jesus choose the twelve apostles? "He appointed twelve—designating them apostles—that they might be with him and that he might send them out to preach" (Mark 3:14).

Jesus chose these men to be *with* Him. This was not a revolutionary idea in His day, for there are numerous instances in the Old Testament where men were trained for the work of God by association with other men of God.

God had the prophet Elijah choose Elisha to help him and carry on after he was gone. Elijah did not find him in the schools of the prophets, studying and meditating, but in the field working (1 Kings 19:15-16,19). The disciples also were called from their daily work to go to be with Jesus (Matt. 4:18-22; 9:9).

Elijah did not beg Elisha to go with him, or use his prophetic office to force him against his will into the ministry. Every person must count the cost and enter into discipleship training willingly. In fact, from the record of their discussion, it appears that Elijah was perfectly willing to let Elisha bow out if he wanted to. If he was to collaborate with him, he must learn from him voluntarily (1 Kings 19:19-21).

It cost Elisha something to follow Elijah. With the evil Queen Jezebel on the rampage in Israel, the northern kingdom, these were, no doubt, uncertain times for the prophet of God and anyone associated with him. Had Elisha consulted with flesh and blood, he would have undoubtedly received counsel to stay with his oxen in the field; it was far safer and much more lucrative.

But Elisha was aware of the tremendous spiritual enrichment that would be his if he spent time with the mighty prophet of God. So after he made the break and killed his oxen, his means of livelihood—a final act of total commitment—and went with Elijah (1 Kings 19:21), what did he find himself doing? Serving Elijah. It is true that those who would lead must first learn to serve. And it is equally true that to train men a person must be willing to spend time with those men in hours of conversation and association in the normal affairs of life.

That is one reason why you cannot take on too many men at once. You can spread yourself too thin and never get any quality time with any of them. You only have so much emotional reserve, so you are limited in the number of men you can train by the hours in a day and the spiritual and emotional capacity of your own life. A common mistake is to try to do too much, too quickly, and with too many.

We learn from the association of these two men that Elijah never urged Elisha to continue with him in the work. Quite the contrary. On three occasions Elijah encouraged Elisha to reevaluate their relationship and leave if he wanted to, but three times Elisha refused. Elijah had made the right choice. At Gilgal, Bethel, and Jericho Elisha was given the opportunity to quit, but he chose to stay by Elijah's side (2 Kings 2:1-6).

When Elisha decided to follow Elijah and minister to him, it was a decision that stuck. He had counted the cost and determined that this was for him. So in your choice of men and subsequent association with them in the ministry, it is imperative that you allow those men to get the mind of God on the matter, to know exactly what's involved, and to realize that your getting together is not primarily for *your* benefit but for theirs.

The association of Moses and Joshua is another illustration of this point. God had given Joshua to Moses in answer to Moses' prayer and one of the first things Moses did was put some of his honor on Joshua (Num. 27:15-20). That's an important point. I have talked with men who were afraid to train other men as spiritual leaders in the congregation for fear of losing some of the loyalty or respect of the people. They enjoyed being the center of attention; they enjoyed the feeling of having the people dependent on them and them alone. Moses shared his authority with Joshua.

As we watch Moses in this context, we notice that he found his security in God. He rejoiced to see Joshua begin to carry some of the load. In their association, Joshua was there to help Moses in the ministry and carry on after he was gone. He succeeded to the leadership some years later. "Now it came about after the death of Moses the servant of the Lord that the Lord spoke to Joshua the son of Nun, Moses' servant, saying, 'Moses My servant is dead; now therefore arise, cross this Jordan, you and all this people, to the land which I am giving to them, to the sons of Israel" (Josh. 1:1-2).

The Old Testament gives ample evidence that on-the-job training was not a new idea in Jesus' day. When Jesus approached the twelve disciples with the idea, they knew what it was all about and rejoiced at the opportunity. They had no idea of *all* that would be involved, but no doubt were delighted and honored to be chosen. Later, as Christianity developed under their leadership, the procedure was continued.

Peter had men with him when he went to the home of Cornelius at the invitation of the men whom the centurion had sent. "The Spirit told me to have no hesitation about going with them. These six brothers also went with me, and we entered the man's house" (Acts 11:12).

Later the apostle Paul carried on this ministry of training by association. "He was accompanied by Sopater son of Pyrrhus from Berea, Aristarchus and Secundus from Thessalonica, Gaius from Derbe, Timothy also, and from the province of Asia, Tychicus and Trophimus" (Acts 20:4).

When he wrote this last letter to Timothy, Paul reminded him of some of the things he had endeavored to impart. "You, however, know all about my teaching, my way of life, my purpose, faith, patience, love, endurance" (2 Tim. 3:10).

The effect this ministry of making disciples by association has on the men in training is powerful, dramatic, and life changing. It is almost unbelievable to see the transformation that took place in the lives of the twelve apostles. It is one of the most spectacular miracles in Scripture. To watch them go from the humble shores of Galilee to the sophisticated center of Jerusalem and more than hold their own with the most august assembly Jerusalem could produce is a wonder to behold.

The Old Testament records an equally amazing phenomenon. David watched as a rag-tag, discouraged, discontented band of men joined themselves to him and he became a captain over them. After a short time they began to change. In their association with David and their serving under him, they became the truly great men of their day. Some of David's spirit rubbed off on them.

They were transformed into brave, heroic warriors whose exploits are legend. The Bible tells us, "Now these are the heads of the mighty men whom David had, who gave him strong support in his kingdom, together with all Israel, to make him king, according to the word of the Lord concerning Israel" (1 Chron. 11:10). The rest of that chapter records the exploits of these strong, valiant, courageous men. The change that came into their lives as they held strongly with David in his kingdom is nothing short of miraculous.

Every pastor has in his congregation men who today are merely spectators in the kingdom of God, but who would pay any price to be involved with him in the real heart of the ministry. But it will cost *him*. Such men need his sermons and instruction, but he will have to share his life with them. And that costs. The apostle John said, "This is how we know what love is: Jesus Christ laid down his life for us. And we ought to lay down our lives for our brothers" (1 John 3:16).

Is it worth it? What are the dividends of this kind of ministry?

Jesus ordained twelve men that they should be in association with Him and that He might send them forth to preach. He had two things in mind in the training of the Twelve. One, that they would be of help to Him then and there in carrying out His mission. Two, that they would carry on after He was gone.

He would send them forth to preach to the high council of the Jews, to the philosophers of Athens, to the worshipers of idols, to the wild barbarians, to Roman soldiers—to anyone and everyone who would listen. He knew His training had to be in depth because these men would face formidable opposition. They would be stoned in the streets, beaten badly, and thrown into prison. So their preparation was vital. Shallow training and halfhearted commitment would not stand the test. They were saved to save others, but it would be a rough and rocky road most of the way.

The Principle of Instruction

In addition to His making His men His disciples by being with them in the everyday work of the ministry, Jesus also had special times of instruction with them. He told them, "The secret of the kingdom of God has been given to you. But to those on the outside everything is said in parables" (Mark 4:11).

And they knew what they were in for. "I am sending you out like sheep among wolves. Therefore be as shrewd as snakes and as innocent as doves. But be on your guards against men; they will hand you over to the local councils and flog you in their synagogues. On my account you will be brought before governors and kings as witnesses to them and to the Gentiles" (Matt. 10:16-18).

They knew it was not going to be as easy as an outing in the park. Jesus prepared them to face opposition and rejection. "If any place will not welcome you or listen to you, shake the dust off your feet when you leave, as a testimony against them" (Mark 6:11).

It is well that men do not enter discipleship training with their heads in the clouds. It is interesting to note that when Jesus chose Paul, He gave him a glimpse through Ananias of what was waiting for him down the road. Speaking to Ananias for transmission to Paul, Jesus said, "This man is my chosen instrument to carry my name before the Gentiles and their kings and before the people of Israel. I will show him how much he must suffer for my name" (Acts 9:15-16).

When you are training potential disciples and workers, let them in on some of the trials and tribulations of the ministry that you have faced. Talk to them about some of the times you were rejected while witnessing in the neighborhood. Tell them about the cost of discipleship.

Dawson Trotman, founder of The Navigators, used to take a few of us aside and tell us about his defeats as well as his victories. But he was also careful to help us see that the mighty hand of God was always there to see us through. A verse he delighted to share with us was, "'No weapon that is formed against you shall prosper; and every tongue that accuses you in judgment you will condemn. This is the heritage of the servants of the Lord, and their vindication is from Me,' declares the Lord" (Isa. 54:17).

Jesus told His men, "You did not choose me, but I chose you to go and bear fruit—fruit that will last. Then the Father will give you whatever you ask in my name" (John 15:16).

His training was out where the battle raged. Occasionally He would take His men aside for some special times together, but His training was mostly "on the job." They were in the ministry with Him. John looked back with awe and wonder at what he had experienced. "That which was from the beginning, which we have heard, which we have seen with our eyes, which we have looked at and our hands have touched—this we proclaim concerning the Word of life. The life appeared; we have seen it and testify to it, and we proclaim to you the eternal life, which was with the Father and has appeared to us" (1 John 1:1-2).

Jesus was available to His men. The Eternal Word became audible, visible, and touchable. They were close to Him. They were chosen to be with Him, but always for the grand purpose of preparing them for their ministry. He designed His training so that their lives should bring forth lasting fruit. He did not prepare them to go out to a life of secluded fellowship with one another, so He did not prepare them in a secluded fellowship.

I have made mistakes in this regard. I have tried to train men by gathering them together in a quiet basement once a week to discuss the Christian life and then supplement this with occasional seminars or special meetings. It didn't work. But men who have ministered with me in the push and shove of life, out where we face victory and defeat daily, out in the world of real living, are today productive for Christ. I have watched them bear fruit that remains.

In summary, three things are a must for the person who would help others become stalwart, loyal, productive disciples in the ministry of Jesus Christ.

1. He must have clearly in mind what he wants them to know and understand of the things of God; he must know what are the basic ingredients in a life of discipleship.

2. He must have a clear picture of what he wants these disciples to become. He must know what bedrock elements of Christian character must be theirs and what kind of people they should be.

3. He must have a vivid vision of what he wants them to learn to do and a workable plan to help them accomplish it.

In this chapter we have seen the approach of Jesus Christ, His apostles, and the prophets of the Old Testament in carrying out this ministry. They selected their followers carefully; they utilized the "with him" principle—the concept of association and example; and they had specific times of solid, clear, plain instruction.

Now the exciting thing is this. None of these is beyond the reach of the ordinary Christian. We can all share with others what we have learned. And we can pray that our lives will be an example to others to help them grow in their devotion to Christ and in their effectiveness in His cause.

CHAPTER 3

MAKING DISCIPLES
IN THE EARLY CHURCH

"They devoted themselves to the apostles' teaching and to
the fellowship, to the breaking of bread and to prayer"
(Acts 2:42).

My dad was a master carpenter. He built many of the houses in
the community where I was born. He was a highly skilled
craftsman and did excellent work. However, none of his abilities rubbed off on me. I have worked on a carpentry crew, but
never quite got the hang of it. In fact, I still am not sure how the
builders do it. It amazes me to watch a building go up and see
how much time and attention is given to the foundation. It
seems the construction crew never gets started with the building itself. Sometimes they spend months on just the hole in the
ground. The bigger the building, the more time they spend
working on the base that will support the superstructure.

Nearly two thousand years ago, Jesus Christ began a
movement that was to spread to the ends of the earth. His
gospel was to go to the noblest king and to the humblest
worker. It would encompass the whole world. It was designed
to reach the world with the Good News that salvation had come
to men.

The Example and Commission of Jesus

Jesus Christ began His mission with a personal ministry of a
little more than three years. One of the key aspects of that time
was His training of the twelve disciples, whom He named
apostles. That training was the foundation of His whole minis-

try. Much of His time during those three-plus years was concentrated on these men. He knew that in order for His mission to succeed, much would depend on the dedication, loyalty, courage, and faith of the men whom He had chosen and trained.

The importance of this approach was first impressed on my mind when I was a young Christian. I had gone to a Christian conference and in one of the messages the speaker was emphasizing how vital these men were to Jesus' mission. He told us a story that stirred our imaginations. He spoke of the return of Jesus to heaven—His ascension—and the excitement that it caused among the angels. He painted quite a picture, for he was good with words.

He told of one of the angels who asked the returned Son of God a question, "What plan do You have to continue the work You began on earth?"

Without hesitation Jesus answered, "I left it in the hands of the apostles."

Another angel asked, "What if they fail?"

Again there was no hesitation, "I have no other plan."

The speaker assured us it was only a story, but it got the point across. The future of Christianity, humanly speaking, rose or fell on the ministry of these men.

Jesus' last words to His disciples were, "You will receive power when the Holy Spirit comes on you; and you will be my witnesses in Jerusalem, and in all Judea and Samaria, and to the ends of the earth" (Acts 1:8). The words *you will be my witnesses* are the key to the perpetuation of Jesus' mission in the Book of Acts. The strategy of outreach was to go first to Jerusalem, then Judea and Samaria, and finally to the ends of the earth.

What must the apostles' responses to that commission have been? What was in their thinking? It certainly must have crossed their minds that Jesus' mission to them was indeed a big job. It was a big world with many people and many languages. Who among them know how to speak to a Parthian or to a Mede? Did anyone know the languages of Mesopotamia and Cappadocia?

If they were concerned about that, they shouldn't have been. Jesus, as always, had a plan. He had told His disciples that they should not leave Jerusalem, "but wait for the gift my Father promised, which you have heard me speak about. For John baptized with water, but in a few days you will be baptized with the Holy Spirit" (Acts 1:4-5).

The Day of Pentecost

The promise of the coming of the Holy Spirit was fulfilled ten days after the ascension. "When the day of Pentecost came, they were all together in one place. Suddenly a sound like the blowing of a violent wind came from heaven and filled the whole house where they were sitting. They saw what seemed to be tongues of fire that separated and came to rest on each of them. All of them were filled with the Holy Spirit and began to speak in other tongues as the Spirit enabled them" (Acts 2:1-4).

During the Feast of Pentecost—as with other popular Jewish feasts—Hebrew men from every nearby nation would come to Jerusalem. They would stay for the feast, rejoice in the goodness and blessing of God, and depart. This particular feast was no exception, but it did contain a few surprises.

The apostles, as a result of their lives being filled with the Holy Spirit and their subsequent ability to communicate in languages other than their own, were in the streets of Jerusalem preaching the gospel.

> Now there were staying in Jerusalem God-fearing Jews from every nation of the world. When they heard this sound, a crowd came together in bewilderment, because each one heard them speaking in his own language. Utterly amazed, they asked, "Are not all these men who are speaking Galileans? Then how is it that each of us hears them in his own native language? Parthians, Medes and Elamites; residents of Mesopotamia, Judea and Cappadocia, Pontus and Asia, Phrygia and Pamphylia, Egypt and the parts of Libya near Cyrene; visitors from Rome (both Jews and converts to Judaism); Cretans and Arabs—we hear them declaring the wonders of God in our own tongues!" (Acts 2:5-11).

The people in Jerusalem were amazed. Many of them had come to scores of feasts through the years and had never seen or heard anything like this. Some accused the apostles of drunkenness. With that Peter stood up and preached the first sermon recorded in the Book of Acts.

He began by quoting a passage of Scripture in answer to his detractors. Here was this plain-spoken Galilean fisherman, standing in the center of Jerusalem, lifting up his voice and making the old streets ring with the message of the risen Christ. How did it occur to him to answer those mockers with a quotation from Scripture? The answer is obvious. He had walked for over three years with Jesus, and had seen Him answer His critics many times. He had spent over three years with the One who frequently quoted the Bible. Peter had learned his lesson well and now quoted the Prophet Joel (2:28-32).

Then Peter got right into the crux of the issue—the message of the gospel.

> Men of Israel, listen to this: Jesus of Nazareth was a man accredited by God to you by miracles, wonders and signs, which God did among you through him, as you yourselves know. This man was handed over to you by God's set purpose and foreknowledge; and you, with the help of wicked men, put him to death by nailing him to the cross. But God raised him from the dead, freeing him from the agony of death, because it was impossible for death to keep its hold on him (Acts 2:22-24).

He preached a crucified and risen Christ, supporting what he said with Scripture.

The results were startling: "When the people heard this, they were cut to the heart and said to Peter and the other apostles, 'Brothers, what shall we do?'" (Acts 2:37).

The test of any message is not whether it is a good or bad sermon, but whether God uses it. Is the blessing of God on it? Here God blessed tremendously as three thousand people responded to the gospel (Acts 2:41).

Then follows one of the most interesting statements in Scripture. "They [the converts] devoted themselves to the apostles' teaching and to the fellowship, to the breaking of bread and to prayer" (Acts 2:42).

What makes this passage so fascinating is what is *not* recorded. What happened between verses 41 and 42? How did the apostles go about getting all those people together in a devoted fellowship? Have you ever tried to have a meeting for new converts after an evangelistic thrust or a special meeting? How many of them showed up? Usually not too many. But the apostles, having been trained by Jesus, were able to do it.

The Ministry of Follow-up

Here were the apostles with three thousand converts on their hands. What were most of these people planning to do? Probably what they had always done—enjoy the feast and go home, scattering to the four winds. But the apostles had other plans.

What was their commission? Get converts? No. Their commission (and ours) was to *make disciples* (Matt. 28:19). Jesus had been clear about that, and these men had heard Him talk about discipleship many times. They knew His standards and what He expected from His followers.

The standards of Jesus.

> If you remain in me and my words remain in you, ask whatever you wish, and it will be given you. This is to my Father's glory, that you bear much fruit, showing yourselves to be my disciples (John 15:7-8).

> To the Jews who had believed him, Jesus said, "If you hold to my teaching, you are really my disciples. Then you will know the truth, and the truth will set you free" (John 8:31-32).

> A new commandment I give you: Love one another. As I have loved you, so you must love one another. All men will know that you are my disciples if you love one another (John 13:34-35).

> If anyone comes to me and does not hate his father and mother, his wife and children, his brothers and sisters—yes, even his own life—he cannot be my disciple. And anyone who does not carry his cross and follow me cannot be my disciple (Luke 14:26-27).

> In the same way, any of you who does not give up everything he has cannot be my disciple (Luke 14:33).

The plan of Jesus. So what were the apostles to do with the converts? Just stand there while these three thousand new believers casually walked out of town? Hardly.

On another occasion after the resurrection Jesus had asked Peter some rather piercing questions.

> When they had finished eating, Jesus said to Simon Peter, "Simon son of John, do you truly love me more than these?"
>
> "Yes, Lord," he said, "you know that I love you."
>
> Jesus said, "Feed my lambs."
>
> Again Jesus said, "Simon son of John, do you truly love me?"
>
> He answered, "Yes, Lord, you know that I love you."
>
> Jesus said, "Take care of my sheep."
>
> The third time he said to him, "Simon, son of John, do you love me?"
>
> Peter was hurt because Jesus asked him the third time, "Do you love me?" He said, "Lord, you know all things; you know that I love you."
>
> Jesus said, "Feed my sheep" (John 21:15-17).

What Jesus told Peter primarily was to feed the lambs and the sheep. So here were three thousand lambs, newly born into the kingdom of God. And Jesus' mandate was that they must be fed and they must be discipled.

The activities of the apostles. In order to provide food and housing for those who needed to be fed and discipled, those who originally had no intention of staying in Jerusalem for any length of time, the apostles took some emergency measures. These would enable the new believers to stay and receive the follow-up training and help they would need.

> All the believers were together and had everything in common. Selling their possessions and goods, they gave to anyone as he had need. Every day they continued to meet together in the temple courts. They broke bread in their homes and ate together with glad and sincere hearts, praising God and enjoying the favor of all the people. And the Lord added to their number daily those who were being saved (Acts 2:44-47).

During the next series of accounts in the Book of Acts, these new converts are not very visible. But they must have been just like young children in a family, watching everything, hearing everything, and soon to imitate everything. Their numbers began to grow; at one time five thousand men were added (Acts 4:4). Later, additional multitudes were reached (Acts 5:14).

Examples to the new believers. As thousands were being

swept into the kingdom, what was going on in the lives of the new converts? They were watching as the apostles were beaten, threatened, and hauled off to jail for their testimony for Christ (Acts 4:17, 5:18,40). They observed as the apostles preached the gospel at every opportunity (Acts 3:14-15; 4:10,33; 5:30-31).

They were there as the apostles responded with joy to the persecution they were forced to endure. "So they went on their way from the presence of the Council, rejoicing that they had been considered worthy to suffer shame for His name" (Acts 5:41, NASB). And they listened carefully as the apostles diligently taught them the things of the Lord. "Day after day, in the temple courts and from house to house, they never stopped teaching and proclaiming the good news that Jesus is the Christ" (Acts 5:42).

What effect did this have on the lives of these growing disciples? What lessons were they learning? The answers become obvious as we see them become functioning disciples and workers in the body of Christ. The training they received from the apostles sank in. They were like tape recorders with the recording mechanism turned on. Soon they would begin to play it back to the world.

The hour of testing. Then came the hour in which they were tested. After the death of Stephen, a tremendous persecution came against the believers. "On that day a great persecution broke out against the church at Jerusalem, and all except the apostles were scattered throughout Judea and Samaria" (Acts 8:1).

It is interesting to note that this event is the next step in the fulfillment of the commission given earlier (Acts 1:8). Notice that all were dispersed except the apostles. Why weren't they scattered? Because they had been granted religious asylum by Gamaliel, who had declared, "Leave these men alone! Let them go! For if their purpose or activity is of human origin, it will fail. But if it is from God, you will not be able to stop these men; you will only find yourselves fighting against God" (Acts 5:38-39).

The religious leaders had agreed to this, but there was no protection for the ordinary believers. So they fled, but not in a panic. "Therefore they that were scattered abroad went everywhere preaching the Word" (Acts 8:4, KJV).

Why did they do that? Why did they go everywhere preaching the Word? Because they had been raised in an atmosphere of witnessing. They assumed that it was the normal thing to do. It was all they knew of Christianity. They had been taught it and had been given examples.

As we think of our ministry of making disciples today, we need to take this point seriously. If we want to see a certain performance or certain attitude develop in those with whom we are working, we must remember the tremendous power of the personal example. These new Christians were merely following the example of their leaders.

The ministry of Philip. The Spirit of God then directs our attention to one of these men, a deacon. "Philip went down to a city in Samaria and proclaimed the Christ there" (Acts 8:5). We see him preaching the name of Christ in the area, resulting in "great joy in that city" (Acts 8:8).

Later, we see him witnessing to the man in the chariot. "Then Philip began with that very passage of Scripture and told him the good news about Jesus" (Acts 8:35). Again, it was what had been shown him and taught him that made him an effective witness. His training had prepared him for this responsibility.

Others' ministries. Some of those people who had been in Jerusalem on the day of Pentecost were from Cyrene (Acts 2:10). Some of them had responded to the gospel and had received discipleship training from the apostles. After they were scattered by the persecution, they reappear again.

> Now those who had been scattered by the persecution in connection with Stephen traveled as far as Phoenicia, Cyprus and Antioch, telling the message only to Jews. Some of them, however, men from Cyprus and Cyrene, went to Antioch and began to speak to Greeks also, telling them the good news about the Lord Jesus. The Lord's hand was with them, and a great number of people believed and turned to the Lord (Acts 11:19-21).

We see them, too, out preaching the Lord Jesus. Their testimony was powerful, as the hand of the Lord was on their lives. Their message was simple; they preached the Lord Jesus. And many believed.

The continued interest of the apostles. One other thing

needs to be noted in the training of these growing disciples. When they left the apostles, they were not forgotten. The apostles followed them with their prayers and with their concern.

> News of this reached the ears of the church at Jerusalem, and they sent Barnabas to Antioch. When he arrived and saw evidence of the grace of God, he was glad and encouraged them all to remain true to the Lord with all their hearts. He was a good man, full of the Holy Spirit and faith, and a great number of people were brought to the Lord (Acts 11:22-24).

A great principle of training emerges here. These people were out of sight, but not out of mind. When it became evident that they needed help in their ministry, they received it.

Summary and application. As we have reviewed the apostles' ministry after the ascension of Jesus and the subsequent ministry of those disciples whom they trained, we see so much that is applicable to our own lives and ministries. Pastors have asked me, "But do you think this discipleship training can work in the church today?"

My answer has always been the same: It worked in the church in Jerusalem; it worked in the church in Antioch. This whole approach got its start in the New Testament church. It grew and flourished in these churches. *And there is no reason on earth why it cannot be applied today.*

The Great Commission remains the same. The message of the gospel is the same. We minister through the power of the same Holy Spirit. We have the same Word of God. And we have the promise Jesus made after the command to make disciples, "And surely I will be with you always, to the very end of the age" (Matt. 28:20).

What then is the problem today? Why don't we see more of this going on? Why are fruitful, dedicated, mature disciples so rare? The biggest reason is that all too often we have relied on programs or materials or some other thing to do the job.

The ministry is to be carried on by people, not programs. It is to be carried out by some*one* and not by some *thing*. Disciples cannot be mass produced. We cannot drop people into a "program" and see disciples emerge at the end of the production line. It takes time to make disciples. It takes individual, personal attention. It takes hours of prayer for them. It takes patience and understanding to teach them how to get into the Word of God for themselves, how to feed and nourish their souls, and by the power of the Holy Spirit how to apply the word to their lives. And it takes being an example to them of all of the above.

The Example of the Apostle Paul

This ministry of making disciples takes time and effort, but the results are lasting. The apostle Paul is an example of what it takes and what the cost of this kind of ministry is.

He had just been on a missionary journey and God had abundantly blessed his efforts. Many had been brought to the Lord. Thousands had heard the gospel. The mission had almost cost him his life. But on that trip, after he had been stoned and left for dead on one occasion, he returned to the very places where the hostility had been the greatest, "strengthening the disciples and encouraging them to remain true to the faith" (Acts 14:22).

He returned to Antioch, and some time passed. Paul became burdened for these people and said to Barnabas, "Let us go back and visit the brothers in all the towns where we preached the Word of the Lord, and see how they are doing" (Acts 15:36). We often refer to this journey as Paul's second mission. Actually this was the beginning of his first *discipling* journey. "He went through Syria and Cilicia, strengthening the churches" (Acts 15:41).

After the long and arduous trip, he returned again to Antioch. The Spirit of God moved in his heart once more, and he went out again on another mission. "After spending some time in Antioch, Paul set out from there and traveled from place to place throughout the region of Galatia and Phrygia, strengthening all the disciples" (Acts 18:23). Yes, it took time and effort, but the apostle Paul was a true maker of disciples.

In a later letter, Paul spells out this aspect of his ministry. Speaking of Jesus he said:

> So, naturally, we proclaim Christ! We warn every-
> one we meet, and we teach everyone we can, all that we
> know about Him, so that, if possible, we may bring every
> man up to his full maturity in Jesus Christ. This is what I

am working at all the time, with all the strength that God
gives me (Col. 1:28-29, *Phillips*).

Note that carefully. He *worked* at it all the time, with all the
strength God gave him. What did he do? He won people to
Christ and brought them to their full maturity in Him. The
process was costly and time consuming. On one occasion he
stated to those who would carry on the ministry, "So be on your
guard! Remember that for three years I never stopped warning
each of you night and day with(Acts 20:31).

He had carried on the same kind of ministry among the
Thessalonians.

> For you know that we dealt with each of you as a
> father deals with his own children, encouraging, comfort-
> ing and urging you to live lives worthy of God, who calls
> you into his kingdom and glory (1 Thess. 2:11-12).

We have looked briefly at the ministry of the apostles whom
Jesus had chosen to carry on His work. Their ministry was set
in the context of prisons, beatings, threatenings, earthquakes,
shipwrecks, plots to murder, miracles, and many other events
up and down the roads and seas of the Mediterranean world.

The devil tried his best to stop them, but they got the job
done. They stuck with it. Their commission had been clear:
"Therefore go and make disciples" (Matt. 28:19). And they did.
They proved to be steadfast, unmoveable, always abounding in
the work the Lord had sent them to do.

CHAPTER 4

PEOPLE HELP PEOPLE

"And I searched for a man among them who should build
up the wall and stand in the gap before Me" (Ezek. 22:30).

In any congregation there is a wide range of interest in the
things of the Lord. Some people are merely spectators in the
crowd, those who just come to watch and listen. They are there
for a variety of reasons: habit, sense of duty, peer pressure, for
business contacts, for social contacts. Some are Christians who
are just going along for the ride. Some are non-Christians who
are just there.

In addition to the spectators, there is also a group of
participants. These people willingly take on some ministry in
the church and, in most cases give it their best. They may serve
as greeters in the Sunday school, ushers in the worship service,
and serve on committees or as officers in the various circles and
groups that meet in the life of the congregation. Some may
teach in the Sunday school or be involved in a variety of service
activities.

These participants are the backbone of the church. It
could not function without them. So when we talk about a
discipleship ministry in the church, we must not overlook or
neglect these people who play such a valuable role. The church
must continue to offer a varied program in which anyone can
feel welcome and be at home; the Sunday school must continue
to function with classes for all ages; other organizations must
provide fellowship for people with their different interests and
needs. Yet in all these programs people are still primary, for

49

ultimately they cannot be helped by some *thing* but must be helped by someone.

During one of our moves we bought a new home that had no lawn; the front and back yards were just bare earth. A friend of ours bought some sod for us, and at the same time our neighbor bought his sod from the same company. When they were both laid, they looked beautiful (so much so that the landscaping company used our two lawns in some of their promotional advertising).

Our neighbor decided to water his lawn with an automatic underground sprinkler system, which he had installed before the lawn was laid. I chose to buy a hose and turn it over to my wife, Virginia. So I had a blonde out there with a hose watering my lawn while my neighbor would merely turn his controls on and off.

After four years my neighbor's lawn returned to its original state—just bare earth covered with weeds. Our lawn was still green and beautiful. What made the difference? Personal care. Whenever Virginia would see a brown spot on the grass, she would give it special attention and more water. With the mechanical system there was no way to give individual care and attention to the grass; as holes in the sprinklers were clogged by dirt and small stones, certain portions of the lawn received no water. Soon the lawn dried up and was destroyed, while ours remained lush and green.

You cannot turn over a lawn to a mechanical system in a dry climate such as ours and expect success. Each blade of grass needs special care. That is much more true with people. Each of us has specific needs and these can only be met by other people. No system or program will automatically meet and cure the needs of human beings. Because we are individuals, we each have specific needs which people alone can meet.

A danger exists here in not recognizing that some people are not ready or want discipleship training. Some pastors, in their newly found desire to have a discipling ministry and their haste to inaugurate it into the life of the church, drive off some good people or make them feel like second-class citizens in the kingdom of God. Often they will rush into it by insisting on unqualified adherence to a very demanding discipleship performance from everyone at once. They don't get it from the people and many of the latter get hurt in the process. To function most effectively, the church must adapt itself to meet the needs of non-Christians, new Christians, lukewarm Christians, and committed Christians in different ways.

To get people involved in a discipleship ministry and to help them become disciples, three things are necessary initially. They must be motivated to become disciples, they must have regular fellowship with Jesus Christ, and they must witness to Him.

Motivation for Discipleship and People Involvement

The first step in forming a band of people who are eager for discipleship training is motivation. They must be motivated in two directions—inward and outward. Inwardly they must be motivated to have fellowship *with* Jesus Christ, and outwardly they must become witnesses *for* Jesus Christ. The whole process should be approached with much prayer and thought, perhaps illustrated by the way a new building project is handled.

Our church became aware of the need of expanding its educational facilities. This need was mentioned from time to time in the Sunday school. Because of growth, we had to shift a few classes around and ours was one of them. Our adult class was not using all its space, so we traded rooms with a larger class. Now this was not done without some prior notice. We discussed it for a few weeks, the need was made clear, and when the day for the change came we were all used to the idea.

At first we felt somewhat uncomfortable in the new classroom, but we soon got used to it. After all, there was a price to pay for progress. The Sunday school was growing and God was blessing.

Then we were informed that a committee had been formed to study the need for more room. It examined all possibilities and alternatives, and the idea of building on to our present facility was mentioned. The exchange of ideas went on for months and from time to time we would get a report of the committee's progress. All along the congregation became more and more aware of the need.

As growth continued, the situation became more desperate, the need for expansion more urgent. Finally the announcement came: we are going to build! A few people were not convinced that was the way to go, but most of us were sure it was the right step. We held an all-church banquet, and during the evening the first opportunity was given for us to make our pledges to the new building. In that one night we went over the top! The people had a mind to give.

Now what would have happened if all of a sudden, out of the clear blue sky, without any prior discussion, during a Sunday morning service, the pastor had handed out the pledge cards and demanded we make our first pledge right then and there? We would have been unprepared and surprised. It would have been a new idea, and most of us have a tendency to resist new things that come on us suddenly. Without the proper preparation, there would not have been a positive response.

To begin a discipleship training ministry in the church takes the same kind of foresight and planning. The key is to do it slowly and not try to do too much with too many too soon. The spectators are still out there and many of them want to remain that way.

To motivate people to discipleship will be an exciting project. In time you will be able to spot those who show an interest in becoming disciples. They will become aware of their own need for spending time in the Word—reading it, studying it, memorizing it—and establishing a daily time of prayer. (More on how to build these into the lives of your disciples in Chapter 5.)

Fellowship with the Lord

When you begin to see some stirrings of interest in the things of God having to do with discipleship among your people, you are then ready to launch another idea planting campaign, this time on the subject of fellowship with the Lord on a regular basis.

Your goal is to see a band of people raised up who have a strong, regular, personal intake of the Word of God and who have an effective prayer life. These are people who are living in vital union with Jesus Christ on a day-by-day basis, and through whose lives the life of Christ is flowing out in redemptive power to others around them.

To accomplish this you must make sure that your people are not dependent for their spiritual food on weekly sermons but are able to feed themselves on a daily basis from the Word.

One spring my family and I were traveling through Florida on our way from Fort Lauderdale to Tampa. As we were driving along, I was impressed by the beauty of the acres and acres of orange groves. As far as the eye could see, there were orange trees loaded with fruit.

We were still in the middle of orange country when we stopped for the night at a motel. The next morning we went down to the restaurant for breakfast and I ordered orange juice with my eggs.

The waitress came back shortly with some sad news. "Sir," she said, "I can't bring you any orange juice. Our machine is broken."

At first I sat there dumbfounded. I knew we were surrounded by millions of oranges and I knew there were oranges in the kitchen (they used orange slices as a garnish on the plates they served). But now that I wanted a glass of orange juice, I could not have it.

I began to reflect on the situation. What was the problem? No orange juice? Hardly. We were in the middle of thousands of gallons of orange juice. The problem was that she had become so dependent on the machine that when it broke down she couldn't serve a glass of orange juice.

Christians are like that sometimes. They may be surrounded by Bibles in their homes, but if something should happen to the pastor or church so that there was no Sunday morning preaching service, they would go without their spiritual food. They would have no nourishment for their souls. If someone is not available to break open the Word of God and feed them, they would go hungry.

The problem is not that there is no spiritual food. The problem is that many Christians do not know how to get it for themselves. They are like babies in a pantry surrounded by all kinds of canned goods—meats, fruits, vegetables. But they would starve to death unless someone opened those cans for them.

Jesus Christ after His resurrection told Peter to feed the lambs and the sheep. Part of that command is to lead the sheep along so that they can feed themselves. When a person comes to Christ, he needs someone to help him learn how to feed himself. And there might be people in the congregation who have never learned how to feed themselves from the Bible.

Our first and foremost responsibility as Christians is to maintain a strong, day-by-day abiding fellowship with the Lord Jesus by feeding on His Word. And we need to help others do the same.

Witnessing for the Lord

To train people to witness is one of the most gratifying and fulfilling aspects of the discipleship ministry. But people will not witness unless they first spend time with Jesus Christ. Two principles must be taught to the people: one, God does it, and two, He uses people.

God does it. The first principle of witnessing is to make people aware of the fact that God does it. Witnessing is not a human invention and it is not carried on in human strength alone.

If we were to look back to the Day of Pentecost and look at Peter preaching his great sermon (Acts 2), what would we see? We'd see his boldness. We'd admire his message as he courageously proclaimed the gospel of Jesus Christ. We would be prone to stand back and declare, "What a man!' But then we would notice what the inspired writer stated was happening after that momentous day, "And the Lord added to their number daily those who were being saved" (Acts 2:47). It wasn't Peter; it was God!

If anything of spiritual value is done in this world, it will be because God did it. We find this to be so throughout the Scriptures, both Old and New Testaments.

This is illustrated in the life of David and his mighty men. One of these men was Eleazar, the son of Dodoi. He was the one who fought the Philistines after the rest of the Israelites had fled, and fought so hard that his hand stuck to the sword. We look at his courage and stamina and admire him as a great warrior in the army of God. And rightly so. But notice these words, "And the Lord brought about a great victory that day" (2 Sam. 23:9-10). The Lord? We thought it was Eleazar. But the writer says it was God.

Shammah, the son of Agee, was another valiant man in David's retinue, and he won a great victory against the Philistines after his people had fled. Again it states after his achievement, "And the Lord brought about a great victory" (2 Sam. 23:11-12). It was God who did it through him.

This is a principle of which people must be convinced if they are to be fruitful, dedicated, lifelong witnesses for Jesus Christ. A proper understanding of this principle takes some of the fear and nervousness out of people witnessing, for it places their confidence in God. He is the one who does it through them.

God uses people. The second principle of witnessing is that God uses people. Christian men and women are His chosen means of spreading the gospel to the people who need to hear the Good News.

One of the most forceful and dramatic illustrations of this principle may be found in the account of the conversion of Cornelius. He was a God-fearing Roman centurion who gave generously to those in need and was a man of prayer. One afternoon he saw a vision in which an angel gave him some instructions, "Your prayers and gifts to the poor have come up as a remembrance before God. Now send men to Joppa to bring back a man named Simon who is called Peter. He is staying with Simon the tanner, whose house is by the sea" (Acts 10:4-6).

When we study this incident we are confronted with a question. Why didn't the angel simply say, "Believe in the Lord Jesus, and you will be saved—you and your household"? (Acts 16:31). Why didn't the angel urge him to "turn to God in repentance and have faith in our Lord Jesus"? (Acts 20:21). After all, he had been on his knees, had given money, and was an honest, devout seeker after God. Why didn't the angel just give him the straight, simple gospel witness?

Instead he left the centurion with a rather complicated set of instructions. What if he forgot the name of the town, or the name of the man, or the name of the man Peter was staying with, what then?

The reason for the angel's not doing any of these things is rather simple. God does not use angels as His witnesses. He uses people.

Just imagine what God could have done to get the Good News of Jesus Christ to a needy world. He could have arranged the stars to spell out John 3:16 in every language on earth for all to see. He could have put an angel into orbit broadcasting the gospel in every language. But He didn't. He chose to use people.

People are God's witnesses, and they become that as a result of abiding in Jesus Christ. Jesus told His disciples, "Remain in me, and I will remain in you. No branch can bear fruit by itself; it must remain in the vine. Neither can you bear fruit unless you remain in me" (John 15:4,5).

Our fruitfulness is the result of abiding in Christ. So fellowship with Christ must come first, for witnessing is not overwork but overflow. It is Christ *through* people to other people. Paul said, "I will not venture to speak of anything except what *Christ* has accomplished *through me* in leading the Gentiles to obey God by what I have said and done" (Rom. 15:18). It was Christ through Paul to others.

The importance of witnessing is taught by many passages in Scripture. Jesus' last words to His disciples on the Mount of Olives were, "You will be my witnesses" (Acts 1:8).

Many years later the apostle Paul, in writing to the church at Rome, told them his life was "set apart for the gospel of God" (Rom. 1:1). He lived his life in that framework—he had been set apart for the gospel.

Where did he get that idea? In his testimony before King Agrippa, he repeated a portion of Christ's first words to him on the Damascus road. Jesus had said, "Now get up and stand on your feet. I have appeared to you to appoint you as a servant and as a witness of what you have seen of me and what I will show you" (Acts 26:16).

It is interesting to note that Christ's last words to the disciples on the Mount of Olives and His first words to the new apostle on the Damascus Road concerned the matter of witnessing. This is what God has on His heart for the people whom He has redeemed. God saved Paul to use him in the grand enterprise of getting out the gospel. He was saved to witness.

Evangelism is what will keep your discipleship program alive. Without it the purposes of God would be thwarted. The people of God are not buckets to be filled with all the riches of

Christ, but they are channels of blessing to take Christ to the world.

Witnessing must be approached with much prayer, thought, and planning and the ones who will do it are your trained mature and dedicated disciples. The opportunities are boundless and the need is overwhelming. But committed disciples, who are fellowshiping with the Lord, can take advantage of those opportunities and meet those needs.

A question I often ask church leaders is this: "What would you rather have in your congregation, one hundred people who are 90 percent committed or ten people who are 100 percent committed?" Your own answer to that question will determine your philosophy of the ministry and how much effort you would be willing to put forth in developing a committed band of spiritually qualified workers for Jesus Christ.

Today we are riding a groundswell of interest in the Bible by the people in our congregations. Many would love to have a personal working knowledge of the Word of God. Many long to be more effective in their witness for Christ. Many more decry their ineffectiveness in prayer. They dream of being stalwart men and women of God—strong in faith, fervent in spirit, deep in their devotion for Christ.

They crowd the bookstores to get the latest from the Christian publishers; they crowd the evangelical seminaries and the Bible institutes for some Bible training; they crowd the seminars and lectures by well-known speakers and visiting lecturers.

But the answers to many of these milling masses, who are clamoring for spiritual reality, could be found in a quiet, solid, ongoing program of discipleship training in their local churches. This is the challenge to today's generation.

CHAPTER 5

THE PROCESS OF MAKING DISCIPLES

> "As you therefore have received Christ Jesus the Lord, so walk in Him, having been firmly rooted and now being built up in Him and established in your faith, just as you were instructed, and overflowing with gratitude" (Col. 2:6-7, NASB).

Visualize a large manufacturing plant in your town or city that produces shoes. The management has invested great sums of money and many man-hours into the plant to produce the finest shoes possible. Money has been spent on salaries for the employees, machinery for shoemaking, and materials from which the shoes are to be made. The plant is now in operation with hundreds of workers scurrying to and fro. Machines are running full blast, and activity is at a maximum.

One day the president asks the production manager, "How many shoes have we produced so far?"

"None," the manager answers.

"None!" the president exclaims. "How long have we been in operation?"

"Two years."

"Two years? And still no shoes?"

"That's right," the manager says, "no shoes, but we are really busy. In fact, we have been so busy that we are all nearly tired out. We've been very active at our jobs."

A diagram of this plant that *didn't* produce shoes would look something like this:

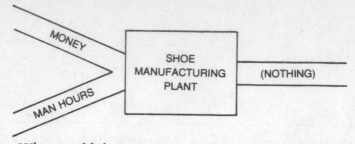

What would the management do in a case like this? Have collective coronaries? Become angry? Concerned? Fire somebody? Try to find out what the problem was? They would probably do all of these things. Because the reason for this factory's existence is to produce shoes. Management wants their investment to pay off and for the plant to look like this:

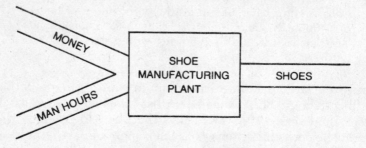

Now let's put a cross on top of that building and transform it into the church on the corner—your church. Again, there is much activity. Men and women are working hard. The budget is higher this year than ever before. The church is very active. The objective, however, is not to produce shoes but disciples. It *should* look like this:

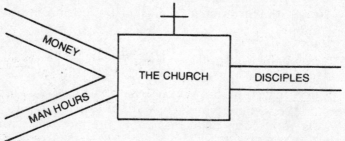

When Dawson Trotman, founder of The Navigators, was trying to recruit counselors for one of the Billy Graham Crusades in a large metropolitan city, he made numerous phone calls to the supporting churches. He would ask them, "Could we have the names of the men and women in your congregation who know their Bibles well enough to lead someone to Christ?"

The church secretary of one of the larger churches replied, "Would you repeat the qualifications again, please?"

Trotman did.

After a long pause, the secretary said rather wistfully, "You know, we did have a man like that in church once, but he moved away."

That church was most likely an exception. But on the other hand, the analysis of Jesus of His own time was, "The harvest is plentiful but the workers are few" (Matt. 9:37). If we're honest with ourselves, we would all sadly admit that it is still the case today. Spiritually qualified workers—disciples who labor hard to make other disciples—are rare.

The Needs of a Convert

For the sake of illustration and simplicity, let's start with a convert. Let's say you've had the joy of leading a person to Jesus Christ. Are you happy? Of course you are. You'd better be. Everybody is happy when a sinner comes to Jesus— heaven rejoices, the convert rejoices, you rejoice. But are you satisfied? No, not yet. You shouldn't be. The commission of Christ to you was to make disciples, not just get converts. So your objective now is to help this new Christian progress to the point where he is a fruitful, mature, and dedicated disciple. You can picture it like this:

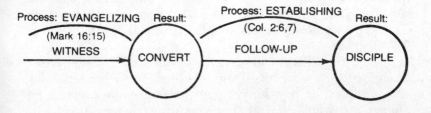

What you need to know is what goes into becoming a disciple for Jesus Christ and then how to help that person get those characteristics built into his life.

The first need a convert has is assurance. He needs to know that he has truly been born again. And if you are to help him, you need to know that too. I have seen people "make decisions," but when I tried to help them grow in grace and in the knowledge of our Lord and Savior Jesus Christ, I discovered that they were still dead in their trespasses and sins. They had no spiritual life. I have learned the hard way that it is impossible to disciple a person who is spiritually dead.

Paul stated, "Therefore, if anyone is in Christ, he is a new creation; the old has gone, the new has come!" (2 Cor. 5:17). In order to identify a genuine convert, you must see in him a change of attitude toward Jesus Christ and a change of attitude toward sin.

This does not mean he now fully understands the doctrine of the lordship of Christ over his life, nor does it mean he has all his old problems solved. But his *basic attitudes* have changed. He now holds Jesus in a *favorable* light (see 1 John 5:11-12) and he is *unfavorable* toward sin (see 1 John 1:9). In other words, he evidences new life.

Another need a convert has is acceptance. He needs two things communicated to him: love and acceptance. They are the two sides of the same coin. Paul set this pattern for us in his attitude toward the Thessalonians. "We loved you so much that we were delighted to share with you not only the gospel of God but our lives as well, because you had become so dear to us" (1 Thess. 2:8).

No wonder these Thessalonians went on so powerfully in their Christian lives and testimonies. "And so you became a model to all the believers in Macedonia and Achaia. The Lord's message rang out from you not only in Macedonia and Achaia—your faith in God has become known everywhere. Therefore we do not need to say anything about it" (1 Thess. 1:7-8).

Paul loved them and had a deep concern for them, so they knew that they were loved and accepted. "You are witnesses, and so is God, of how holy, righteous and blameless we were among you who believed. For you know that we dealt with each of you as a father deals with his own children" (1 Thess. 2:10-11). And when he was absent from them, they were in his thoughts and prayers.

> But, brothers, when we were torn away from you for a short time (in person, not in thought), out of our intense longing we made every effort to see you. For we wanted to come to you—certainly I, Paul, did, again and again—but Satan stopped us. For what is our hope, our joy, or the crown in which we will glory in the presence of our Lord Jesus when he comes? Is it not you? Indeed, you are our glory and joy (1 Thess. 2:17-20).

Paul looked on them as new babes just beginning their spiritual lives. Think about that for a minute. What does a new baby need? Obviously love is at the top of the list. Babies die without it. In a study conducted in a large hospital, the people working in the nursery noticed that the babies who were in the cribs near the door seemed to do better than the ones farther away. They wondered why. After careful study they discovered that the nurses were prone to give the babies near the door more attention as they went about their duties and came in and out of the room. They would pick them up and hug them and speak to them. As we translate that into the spiritual realm, we also discover that spiritual babies need love and acceptance—tender loving care.

The Basic Needs of a Growing Christian

Beside assurance and acceptance, a growing Christian has four basic needs. He needs protection, fellowship, food, and training.

He needs protection. Paul continued to undergo the pains of childbirth for his converts till Christ was formed in them (see Gal. 4:19). He prayed for the Corinthians that they would not do anything wrong (see 2 Cor. 13:7).

New babies need protection. In a hospital nursery the nurses sterilize everything; they wear masks to protect the new little lives from germs. New life is tender and fragile, and must be protected from disease. So it is with new babes in Christ. They need protection from false cults and a variety of attacks by the enemy. People spreading the disease of false religion will show up at their door. The convert's old cronies will try to entice him back into the old paths. A former girlfriend will want to renew the relationship. Satan, as a roaring lion, will try to destroy him. So he must be protected and immunized with the Word of God.

He needs fellowship. He has been born into a family and he needs the fellowship of his brothers and sisters in Christ. When my wife and I came to Christ, a woman in the church we attended took special pains to make sure we met Christian couples our age. She took time to look up passages in the Bible for us in answer to the many questions we had. She would introduce us to others in the congregation who would invite us to their homes for fellowship during the week. A farmer, a banker, a barber—they extended their lives to us and made us feel at home and welcome in the Sunday school and church.

I would still go out with some of my old ex-Marine buddies occasionally, but these people from church stuck with Virginia and me like a peel on an orange. I know our language and lifestyle must have caused them some concern and no doubt even offended some of them, but they overlooked it. Babies occasionally make messes, do foolish things, and may be somewhat of a bother. So are babies in the spiritual realm. Our new friends from church didn't let it bother them, and after some months I noticed something. I felt more at home with these new friends than I did with the people I had known most of my life. The Spirit of God, who had made us part of the body of Christ, was beginning to make us feel part of the body.

When I was in high school, I worked in a bakery. Frequently we would make batches of frosting for cakes and chocolate donuts. I would take great lumps of broken chocolate, put them in a pan, and warm them over a low fire. The chocolate lumps would begin to melt, stick together, and finally blend into one pan full of melted chocolate.

That's what Christian fellowship is all about. Not a group of people in one building like marbles in a bag, but like lumps of chocolate that have blended together and become part of one another. This only happens through the ministry of the Holy Spirit as He slowly warms our hearts together in love, joy, peace, patience, kindness, goodness, faithfulness, gentleness, and self-control (see Gal. 5:22-23).

He needs food. Natural babies need to be fed regularly. Spiritual babies need the same regularity in their feeding. And their spiritual food is the Word of God. "Like newborn babies, crave pure spiritual milk, so that by it you may grow up in your salvation, now that you have tasted that the Lord is good" (1 Peter 2:2-3).

You give the new believer food in two ways. One is to teach him the Word. When my wife and I would visit in the homes of our new Christian friends, the conversation would invariably turn to spiritual things. We would ask questions, and they would get out their Bibles and share the answers with us. I soon became convinced that every answer to every question was in that Book. When they didn't have an answer to a question I asked, they would go to other leaders in the church who would help them with it and they in turn would share that answer with us. I was also learning the Scriptures in Sunday school and church.

But it wasn't till I met Waldron Scott that I learned the second way of feeding on the Word. My friends fed me from the Bible, but Scotty taught me to feed myself. He took Virginia and me through some basic question and answer Bible studies where we had to dig out the answers ourselves. He taught us to memorize Scripture for ourselves. He showed us how we could feed ourselves from the Bible.

So, in order to help a new Christian grow, you must teach him the Word, share it with him, but also teach him how to dig in for himself. Do your best to get him off the spiritual milk bottle. Do your best to help him pass the stage where you have to spoon feed him his spiritual pablum. Teach him to feed himself.

Unless you teach him that vital habit, he will be dependent on others for the rest of his life. God wants him to grow and develop into a strong disciple of Jesus Christ who can, in turn, meet the needs of others and eventually teach them to repeat the process.

He needs training. Again Paul left us an example, "For you know that we dealt with each of you as a father deals with his own children" (1 Thess. 2:11). His example of a father is interesting.

A father does not teach his child everything. He does not

teach him world history or geometry, but he sees to it that his child goes to school. He may turn him over to a swimming instructor to teach him how to swim; he may take him to a soccer coach to teach him to play that sport. Someone else may teach him the art of photography or the techniques of skiing, but the father is responsible for the overall development of the child.

In your training of the new believer, you should focus on the "how to" of things. The answers to "why?" will come later, but at first the new Christian needs to learn *how*. Paul told the Thessalonians, "Finally, brothers, we instructed you *how* to live in order to please God, as in fact you are living. Now we ask you and urge you in the Lord Jesus to do this more and more" (1 Thess. 4:1).

The growing believer needs to learn *how* to have a time of morning prayer and Bible reading, *how* to memorize the Word of God, *how* to do Bible study, *how* to share the gospel in a simple and clear manner. These things will take time, but it is your responsibility to teach them to him.

All of this presupposes that you are doing these things yourself. When Waldron Scott started me on Scripture memory, he told me, "Here's something that has been a great help to me." And he gave me a small packet of verses, the *Beginning with Christ* pack.

What if he had said, "Here's something that will probably be of some help to you. Personally, I have never done it myself"? How would that have impressed me? Not too well.

Being an example is one of the best ways to teach another person. Paul stated, "Whatever you have learned or received or heard from me, or seen in me—put it into practice. And the God of peace will be with you" (Phil. 4:9).

Don Rosenberger was an admiral's writer at Pearl Harbor during World War II. Kenny Watters was a Christian who worked in the same office with Don. After Kenny had led Don to Christ, Don noticed that Kenny came to the office a half hour early, took his Bible out of his desk, and read it before beginning his day's work.

Don assumed that this was what Christians did, so he started coming in half an hour early and reading his Bible.

Then Don noticed that after work Kenny would go out on a hillside, lie down, and pray. So Don began going to the other side of the hill, lying down, and praying as well.

One evening Kenny took him into the mess hall and showed him some charts on the wall. (The chaplain had allowed Kenny to use the mess hall for this purpose.) There were men's names on these charts with Xs and numbers on the lines between the names. Kenny explained that these represented the progress each Christian sailor had made in his Bible study and Scripture memory. He then asked if Don wanted his name on the wall with the others.

"You bet!" Don replied.

When Don saw what these other men were doing, he wanted to do it too. He was motivated by their example and what they were doing, for he knew that these things could be done by others as well. They showed him how to get started, and he was off and running to become the Christian leader he later became.

The Prime Qualities of Growth

If you are to help the new believer grow, you must help him develop two prime qualities in his life. They are a deep desire for fellowship with Jesus Christ and consistency.

Fellowship with Christ. The great hallmark of men and women of God through the ages has been their close walk and intimacy with Jesus Christ. Centuries before Christ, Job declared, "I have not departed from the command of His lips; I have treasured the words of His mouth more than my necessary food" (Job 23:12). You must help build that kind of an attitude into the new Christian's life, so pray that he will long for the Word of God and enjoy it.

You begin by praying for him through verses of Scripture, that their truths might be built into his life. For example:

Monday: "O how I love Thy law! It is my meditation all the day" (Ps. 119:97). Pray, "O Lord, may he love Your law and meditate in it daily."

Tuesday: "Thy testimonies are wonderful; therefore my soul observes them" (Ps. 119: 129). Pray, "Lord, may he consider Your Word wonderful and obey it fully."

Wednesday: "I opened my mouth wide and panted, for I

longed for Thy commandments" (Ps. 119:131). Pray, "May he have this kind of a desire for Your Word."

Thursday: "Thy Word is very pure, therefore Thy servant loves it" (Ps. 119:140). Pray, "Lord, may he have a great love for Your Word."

Friday: "My eyes anticipate the night watches, that I may meditate on Thy Word" (Ps. 119:148). Pray, "May he look forward to nighttime so that he can meditate on Your Word as he goes to sleep."

Saturday: "I rejoice at Thy Word, as one who finds great spoil" (Ps. 119:162). Pray, "O Lord, help him rejoice in Your Word constantly."

You can help him develop this desire for fellowship with Jesus Christ in four ways.

1. Tell him why you yourself have fellowship with Christ daily. Don't major on it as though you have already arrived, but basically tell him *why* you have it, the benefits you have found from this time for your own life, why it has become important to you, and why you have made it a practice to have regular morning Bible reading and prayer. This sharing will take it out of the theoretical realm and put it into the practical. The new Christian will be able to identify with you in these things and see the need for them in his own life.

2. Share some blessings you have gotten from your own time with the Lord. As you meet with the new Christian, share with him some precious truth God has given you from the Word. Share a tasty little morsel that the Lord gave you and pray that his own appetite will be whetted. Share answers to prayer and verses from the Bible that have been a blessing to you.

3. Get him into fellowship with others who are spending daily time with the Lord. Let him meet people who also have a regularity in their fellowship with the Lord. Often a person can be greatly motivated in a group situation when he sees other people who are living the life of discipleship.

I remember the first Navigator rally I attended with Waldron Scott at the Hotel Radisson in Minneapolis. As I walked into the room where the meeting was being held, I was warmly greeted by one of the men on the discipleship team. He took my coat, shook my hand, and pointed me to an usher who took me to a seat.

The meeting began with some lively singing. But there was a difference from the usual song service. If we would sing a song that spoke of the grace of God, the song leader would ask, "Who can quote some verses on the grace of God?" Immediately men and women would be on their feet quoting verses of Scripture, giving references before and after the quotation. The process was repeated for songs on love or God's faithfulness or Christ at Calvary.

I was amazed. I thought, *The room is full of minor prophets!* But then I took a closer look and found most of the people to be college students and working people—folks who were just like me. The speaker then shared with us the need to feed on God's Word and pray. It was a stimulating evening, and God used it to create in me a great desire for fellowship with Himself.

4. Pray for him. The importance of intercessory prayer cannot be overemphasized. The apostle Paul wrote:

> For this reason, since the day we heard about you, we have not stopped praying for you and asking God to fill you with the knowledge of his will through all spiritual wisdom and understanding. And we pray this in order that you may live a life worthy of the Lord and may please him in every way: bearing fruit in every good work, growing in the knowledge of God (Col. 1:9-10).

Waldron Scott had met regularly with me my first two years as a Christian. After I left Minnesota for Seattle to attend the University of Washington, he sent me an old prayer page out of his notebook. (A prayer page is a sheet of paper on which you record specific requests that you have and the answers God sends in answer to the prayers.) For two years my name had been at the top of his daily prayer list.

J. O. Fraser was a missionary in Southwest China, ministering to tribal people living in that very mountainous region. After some years on the field, he noticed a strange thing. The churches which were miles away from the city in which he was living seemed to do better than the church in his own town. He would visit the distant churches occasionally and discovered that they were healthy, active, dedicated, and growing, much more so than the church in which he ministered regularly. Why was that so? Finally the Lord showed him. He found out that he prayed far more diligently for people who were miles away than for those with whom he fellowshiped regularly.

From this discovery he concluded that there were four basic elements in developing disciples and churches: prayer, prayer, prayer, and the Word of God. In thinking through on this, it seems that the thing which does the most good we do least of. It is much easier to talk to men about God than to talk to God about men. Listen to the testimony of Samuel: "Moreover, as for me, far be it from me that I should sin against the Lord by ceasing to pray for you; but I will instruct you in the good and right way. Only fear the Lord and serve Him in truth with all your heart; for consider what great things He has done for you" (1 Sam. 12:23-24).

Consistency. The second prime quality to develop in the life of a new believer is consistency or faithfulness. You must help him see the need for *daily* communion with God, *daily* feeding on the Word. Physically, most of us eat three meals a day. We need a daily intake of protein, fat, and carbohydrates to keep us healthy. We need certain vitamins and minerals too.

So it is spiritually. Since we have been made partakers of the divine nature (see 2 Peter 1:4), that spiritual dimension of our lives now needs regular spiritual nourishment.

But faithfulness cannot be forced. I have tried to force it and failed. In the 1950s I was asked to develop a summer training program for some high school and college students. During the course, my associates and I kept them on a daily schedule of tough spiritual discipline. We demanded they have a quiet time. We required them to memorize a certain number of Bible verses each day. We forced them to do a daily Bible study. We jammed it down their throats. It was mind over matter; we didn't mind and they didn't matter. The whole thing had the air of a Marine Corps boot camp.

After the program was over, many of the young people left the camp disillusioned with these things. We had not yet learned that faithfulness and consistency are the result of the promptings of the Holy Spirit within, not human efforts from outside.

We can help develop this faithfulness in four ways, ways in

which we open the lives of our new Christians to the ministry of the Holy Spirit.

1. Give him small, bite-sized assignments in the Word that you know will be a blessing to him. Many have found the pamphlet *Seven Minutes with God* and the *Devotional Diary* booklet to be one of great help (see Appendix 1). The latter provides a daily Bible reading and space to record the blessings and wonderful things God reveals to his heart.

2. Have a quiet time with him. Call him on the phone and suggest you get together for a brief time of Bible reading and prayer before he and you have to leave for work. Go to his home, have a cup of coffee with him, and spend a little time with the Lord together. Since these things are more easily caught than taught, he will learn from you as he experiences it with you.

In a few days call him and see if he would like to do it again. Then after you think he has caught on to the idea, suggest that you both do it on your own and then meet for lunch to share with one another what you did, how it went, and exchange some blessings that each of you received from your respective times with the Lord.

3. Check up on him and encourage him periodically. This is very important, but the emphasis is on encouragement. During my first year of campus ministry at the University of Pittsburgh, a number of men came to Christ. Whenever I would meet them in the halls of the dorms, I would stop them and check up on them in their Bible study, Scripture memory, and Christian growth.

I soon became known as "Old Mr. Check-up." If they were lagging a bit, they would avoid me. I soon learned it was hard to help a person grow in Christ if he was avoiding me. So I changed and became known as "Mr. Encouragement." The more I encouraged, the more things changed. The new converts grew and we had great fellowship together. They became faithful in their walk with the Lord.

Specifically, what are some of the ingredients that will help a new convert become a dedicated, mature, fruitful disciple of Jesus Christ? And how can we help him get these into his life? In the next chapter we will discuss some of these training objectives, together with some practical activities, tools, and Scripture passages you can use in your discipleship training.

CHAPTER 6

TRAINING OBJECTIVES
FOR A DISCIPLE

"Then they returned to Lystra, Iconium and Antioch, strengthening the disciples and encouraging them to remain true to the faith" (Acts 14:21-22).

Progress. That's what we're dealing with at this stage. We want to help the new Christian advance toward discipleship— growth in grace and in the knowledge of the Lord and Savior Jesus Christ.

This progress cannot be accomplished haphazardly. It has to begin somewhere and then go somewhere, like the educational process from kindergarten to graduation from high school. The student has to master many lessons, assimilate many facts, and learn to do many things. But the way must be planned and organized. A person doesn't learn calculus while playing in the sandbox.

In helping a young Christian grow, you must have a step-by-step building program in mind; you must have certain objectives you want him to attain before he undertakes others. You want to see him go from taking in spiritual milk to partaking of spiritual meat.

In this chapter we want to look at some training objectives which will help make up a life of discipleship. The order in which they have been placed is general, not necessarily sequential. Since every person is a unique individual and must be dealt with as such, the order in which you will present them to the young Christian will vary considerably. You may want to eliminate some and add some. You may want to double the list or cut it in half. The individual needs of the person you are helping will determine the objectives which you will help build into his life and the order which you will follow.

You may not be able to *adopt* some of the things listed here, for the list is simply meant to be a general guide which you can use to stimulate your thoughts and on which you can then improve. But there may be ideas here that you can *adapt* to your own ministry, lifestyle, and needs. The material is presented for your consideration as a suggestion of principles that have worked, not as the law of the Medes and Persians. You may not be able to adopt it all, but there may be some things you can adapt.

These training objectives are designed to stimulate progress on the path of discipleship. In their fulfillment they are characteristics of a disciple's life. To use our illustration, they are the steps in the process of a convert becoming a disciple.

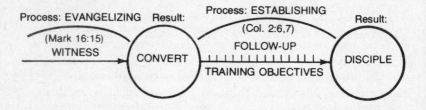

They are written in specific terms. They describe what the person will be doing along the way and how you will know he is doing it. In other words, these objectives are measurable. They will identify the specific attributes of discipleship. They are written to help you measure the progress that is being made. The activities, materials, and Scriptures relate to each training objective. They are listed to give you guidance and direction as you, in turn, provide guidance and direction for the growing Christian.

The purpose of building these objectives into the life of a new believer is that he might be established in the faith. The apostle Paul stated, "As you therefore have received Christ Jesus the Lord, so walk in Him, having been firmly rooted and now being built up in Him and established in your faith, just as you were instructed, and overflowing with gratitude" (Col. 2:6-7, NASB).

A list of the training objectives follows. The details on how they are to be used—their descriptions, activities, helpful materials, Scriptures—are given in Appendix 1. That appendix is an inherent part of this chapter and should be studied carefully.

When these concepts and this material have been shared with pastors, they found the specific training objectives to be very helpful. They are biblical, have been tested in many different situations, and are applicable to life. As you read this chapter and Appendix 1, become aware that these characteristics are at the heart of a person becoming a disciple.

Training Objectives

The following training objectives are listed here and described in detail in Appendix 1.

1.	Assurance of Salvation	16.	Faith
2.	The Quiet Time	17.	Love
3.	Victory over Sin	18.	The Tongue
4.	Separation from Sin	19.	The Use of Time
5.	Christian Fellowship	20.	The Will of God
6.	The Bible	21.	Obedience
7.	Hearing the Word	22.	The Holy Spirit
8.	Reading the Word	23.	Satan—Know Your Enemy
9.	Bible Study	24.	Dealing with Sin
10.	Scripture Memory	25.	Assurance of Forgiveness
11.	Meditation on the Word	26.	Second Coming of Christ
12.	Application of the Word	27.	Witnessing
13.	Prayer	28.	Follow-up
14.	Personal Testimony	29.	Giving
15.	Lordship of Christ	30.	World Vision

These are thirty vital areas that, when built into a life, make up the profile of a disciple. As mentioned before, depending on the needs of the person with whom you are working, you may add to this list or eliminate some of the topics.

With one person, love (No. 17) may be the great need in his life and you'll want to deal with it early. With another, the need may be obedience (No. 21) and you'll have to begin with that topic. For the sake of illustration, two of the topics will now be commented on in greater detail—the personal testimony (No. 14) and application of the Word (No. 12).

The Personal Testimony

One of the most helpful things a young Christian can do is write out his personal testimony. This exercise will help him think through in his own mind what God has done in his life and will prepare him to share his story simply and clearly with others.

Sharing how you became a Christian is one of the best ways of witnessing. It is particularly helpful in presenting Jesus Christ to relatives and close friends, usually the most difficult people to whom to witness.

In sharing the story of your experience:

1. Make it personal—don't preach. Tell what Christ has done for *you*. Use the pronouns "I," "me," "my," and "mine."

2. Make it short. Three or four minutes should be enough time to deal with the essential facts.

3. Keep Christ central. Always highlight what *He* has done for you.

4. Use the Word of God. A verse or two of Scripture will add power to your story. Remember that the word of God has a keen cutting edge (see Eph. 6:17).

Try writing down your personal testimony just the way you'd tell it to an unbeliever. Make the story of your conversion so clear that another person hearing it would know how to receive Christ.

Tell a little about your life before you trusted Jesus Christ; then tell about your conversion, how you came to trust Him , and something of what it has meant to know Him—the blessings of sins forgiven, assurance of eternal life, and other ways your life or outlook has changed. If you have been a Christian for some time, be sure that your testimony includes some current information about the continuing effect of Jesus Christ in your life.

As you prepare your story, ask the Lord to give you opportunities to share it. Pray for two or three people whom you would particularly like to tell about Jesus Christ in your neighborhood, at work, or at school. Then take the first opportunity to share your testimony with them.

Follow a format similar to this:

MY TESTIMONY

Before I trusted Christ:

How I trusted Christ:

Since I've trusted Christ:

In conclusion, remember that you do not have the power in yourself to convince anyone of spiritual truth. The Holy Spirit convicts non-Christians of their need to know Christ (see John 16:8). As you pray for those with whom you desire to share your personal testimony, be sure to ask God to honor the proclamation of His Word, to convince people of their need, and to strengthen you as you share the gospel.

God has summoned each Christian to be a witness of what he has "seen and heard" (1 John 1:3). Witnessing is a style of living—you are a witness at all times. Loving others and showing your genuine concern for them are practical ways to communicate the love of Christ. You also witness by your life. Actions are often more revealing than words. Your actions, however, are not sufficient to communicate to another the message of the gospel of Christ. You need to witness by your words—to identify openly with Jesus Christ and to tell others how they can be reconciled to God. One of the most effective means of communicating this to another person is the story of how God has worked in your life—your personal testimony.[1]

Application of the Word

Dwight L. Moody said that the Word of God was not given primarily to increase our knowledge, but to guide our steps. Some years ago I read in *Translation*, the magazine of the Wycliffe Bible Translators, something that was so meaningful to me that I wrote it in the back of my Bible. It concerned the application of the Word of God.

> A notable commentary on the practical effects of Bible reading were the simple remarks of Moran, chief of the Piro tribe of jungle Indians of western South America.

He said, "When my wife does something wrong, I say to her, 'Mena, God's Word says so and so,' and she says, 'Moran is that what God's Word says?' So I give her the Word and she reads it for herself and then she doesn't do that anymore. When I do something I shouldn't, she says to me, soft and meek like she always is, 'Moran, doesn't God's Word say so and so?' So then I go and read it and by God's help I don't do that anymore."

Applying the Word of God is taking a portion of Scripture that speaks to your heart, meditating on it, and developing practical steps toward making it an integral part of your life. The following four simple steps outline the way to develop your application on the verse or passage you choose.

1. What does this passage say to me?
2. Where am I falling short?
3. Give specific examples.
4. What am I going to do about it?

This approach takes the Bible out of the theoretical and places the emphasis on daily life where it should be. But all too often the truths of the Word of God are left in the same categories as are other things we admire and appreciate. We are charmed, for example, by the majesty, beauty, and eternity of the Scriptures. But was that God's full intent when He gave us the Bible? Note what Paul says, "All Scripture is God-breathed and is useful for teaching, rebuking, correcting and training in righteousness, so that the man of God may be thoroughly equipped for every good work" (2 Tim. 3:16-17). Scripture must be applied to life.

It is God's desire that His Word be lived out in the daily affairs of life, that the Word of God become flesh and blood and find expression in His people. His desire is that we be walking, living Bibles, demonstrating the beauty and validity of the Scriptures in the home, the plant, the office, the school, the shipyard, the store, or wherever else we might live and work.

Shortly after I became a Christian, I was made aware of this concept and was challenged to make personal applications as part of my weekly Bible study. One of the first books I studied was Paul's letter to the Colossians. As I was studying chapter three, the Holy Spirit caught my attention with this: "But now you must rid yourselves of all such things as these:

anger, rage, malice, slander, filthy language" (Col. 3:8).

I tried to slide past this verse, but the Spirit kept bringing me back to the words "put off anger" (KJV). At the time I had a violent temper, and whenever it flared up I would haul off and bash my fist into the nearest door. In spite of the fact that I often bloodied my knuckles and on one occasion had completely smashed a beautiful diamond and onyx ring my wife had given me, I couldn't seem to stop. And yet here was God's Word: "Put off anger." It was clear to me that this was not just some good advice given to the people at Colossae centuries ago. It was God speaking to me at that moment.

So that week I made a covenant with God. He had spoken to me about my sin of anger, and I promised the Lord I was going to work on it. It was obvious to me that I was falling short of keeping this command. My broken ring lying in a box on the dresser was a clear reminder. So the question became—what was I going to do about this sin in my life?

My first step was to memorize the verse and review it daily for a number of weeks. I prayed and asked the Lord to bring this verse to mind whenever a situation arose where I might be tempted to lose my temper. And I asked my wife to pray for me and remind me of that passage if she saw me failing in my promise to the Lord. So Colossians 3:8 became a part of my life and gradually God removed that sin from me.

The Wheel Illustration

As we look at these training objectives, it is evident that their real purpose is to help us live a Christ-honoring life. In the 1930s, Dawson Trotman, founder of The Navigators, was working with a group of students with a view toward helping them in their Christian lives. He longed to see them progress to maturity, fruitfulness, and commitment. He tried to think of a way to communicate the bedrock essentials of the life that has Christ at the center of all that we are and do.

After a number of unsuccessful attempts the Lord enabled him to design an illustration which communicates the essence of such a life. It shows how Christ should be the center of our lives, that we should live in obedience to Him, communicate with Him through the Word and prayer, and reach out to others through fellowship and witness.

The Wheel Illustration is a helpful way to remember the basic truths about the Spirit-filled life. The key to living that life is Jesus Christ as center and Lord of all you do. With Christ in control, life is balanced and effective.

Christ the Center (2 Cor. 5:17; Gal. 2:20). Just as the driving force in a wheel comes from the hub, so the power to live the Christian life comes from Jesus Christ the Center. He lives in you in the Person of the Holy Spirit, whose expressed purpose is to glorify Christ.

Obedience to Christ (Rom. 12:1; John 14:21). The rim represents the Christian responding to Christ's lordship through wholehearted, day-by-day obedience to Him.

The Word (2 Tim. 3:16; Josh. 1:8). The spokes show the means by which Christ's power becomes operative in your life. You maintain personal contact with God through the vertical spokes—the Word and prayer. The Word is your spiritual food as well as your sword for spiritual battle. It is the foundational spoke for effective Christian living.

Prayer (John 15:7; Phil. 4:6-7). Opposite the Word is the spoke representing prayer. Through prayer you have direct communication with your heavenly Father and receive provision for your needs. As you pray, you show your dependence on and trust in Him.

Fellowship (Matt. 18:20; Heb. 10:24-25). The horizontal spokes concern your relationship to people—believers, through Christian fellowship, and unbelievers, through witnessing. Fellowship centered around the Lord Jesus Christ provides the mutual encouragement, admonition, and stimulation you need.

Witnessing (Matt. 4:19; Rom. 1:16). The first three spokes prepare you for passing on to others all you have received from the Lord. This is accomplished through witnessing, sharing your own experience of Christ and declaring and explaining the gospel, God's power to save.[2]

The Hand Illustration

Another illustration that conveys the importance of the Word of God in the lives of believers and the means to appropriate it practically in their lives is the Hand Illustration. It shows us the five methods of learning from the Bible.

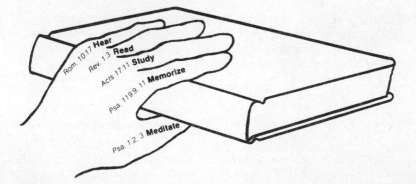

The five means of taking in the Word of God are hearing, reading, studying, memorizing, and meditating.

Hearing the Word of God (Objective No. 7). Hearing the Word from godly pastors and teachers provides us insight into others' study of the Scriptures as well as stimulating our own appetites for the Word.

Reading the Word of God (Objective No. 8). Reading the Bible gives us an overall picture of God's Word. Many find helpful a daily reading program which takes them systematically through the Bible.

Studying the Word of God (Objective No. 9). Studying the Scriptures leads us into personal discoveries of God's truths. Writing down these discoveries helps us organize and remember them better.

Memorizing the Word of God (Objective No. 10). Memorizing God's Word enables us to use the sword of the Spirit to overcome Satan and temptation and to have it readily available for witnessing or helping others with a "word in season."

Meditating on the Word of God (Objective No. 11). Meditation is the thumb of the Word Hand, for it is used in conjunction with each of the other four methods. Only as we meditate on God's Word—thinking of its meaning and application to our lives—will we discover its transforming power at work in us.[3]

Notes

[1]Adapted from "The Spirit-filled Christian," Book 2 of the *Design for Discipleship* series, pp. 44-46. © 1973 by The Navigators and used by permission.

[2]From "The Spirit-filled Christian," Book 2 of the *Design for Discipleship* series, pp. 47-48. © 1973 by The Navigators and used by permission.

[3]From *The Hand* illustration from the Personal Growth Series. © 1976 by The Navigators and used by permission.

CHAPTER 7

THE WORKERS ARE STILL FEW

"When he saw the crowds, he had compassion on them, because they were harassed and helpless, like sheep without a shepherd. Then he said to his disciples, 'The harvest is plentiful but the workers are few. Ask the Lord of the harvest, therefore, to send out workers into his harvest field'" (Matt. 9:36-37).

The commission of Jesus was to make disciples (see Matt. 28:19). He went a step further than just admonishing us to become disciples. So if we are to fall in step with the grand design of God, we must help people become disciples. To stop short of that is to fail to capture the genius of the commission of Christ.

Let's ask again, if you lead a person to Christ, are you happy? Of course you are. You're elated and so is everyone else concerned—the person himself and the angels of God. But are you satisfied? No, you shouldn't be. Jesus told us to do more than just get converts. He told us to make disciples. So you must stick close to the person whom you've led to Christ, and help him grow till he takes his place among those who can vigorously and effectively advance the cause of the Lord. When that happens, he may be considered a mature, committed, fruitful follower of Jesus Christ.

Now, are you happy that your convert has become a disciple? Of course you are. But are you satisfied? No, not if he continues to show a deep interest in helping others to become disciples as well. If that is the case, he is ready to advance to the next stage of usefulness in the kingdom of God; he is ready to become a *worker*.

But there are those who never reach that stage. They are disciples of Jesus Christ in the true sense of the word. They are openly identified with the Lord. They are in fellowship with Him through the Word and prayer. They do manifest the fruit of the Spirit (see Gal. 5:22-23). And they are fulfilling their unique contribution in the body of Christ.

They teach in the Sunday school. They serve on boards and committees and make a valuable contribution, not only by their knowledge of and interest in the matters at hand, but by their godly lives and spiritual depth. But they do not seem to have the gift and calling to become personally and actively involved in a discipleship ministry in the lives of others. To try to push them further in that direction would be a mistake. Disciples—yes! Workers who are actively involved in making disciples—no! Serious damage may be done by overzealous trainers who try to push people too far, beyond the limit of their gifts and calling of God.

It is clear from Scripture that the cause of Christ includes workers of many kinds. What we are aiming at in this chapter and the next two has to do with workers of a *particular* kind. When Jesus stated that the workers were few (Matt. 9:37), He was talking about the worker *directly* involved in the harvest.

I was born and raised on a farm in Iowa. We always had tons of work to do. In wintertime we had to break up the ice in the water tank so the horses and cattle could drink. Fences had to be fixed. Roofs of the house and barns needed repair. We had to vaccinate the pigs, mow the weeds, go to town for new tires for the tractor. Work, work, work.

But at that certain time of year we would look out at our fields and realize that it was time for the harvest. We dropped most of our other work and became *harvest workers*. That is the kind of person Jesus referred to when He stated that the workers were few; He was talking about "harvest workers." These are workers in the kingdom of God who are directly involved in the specific task of reaping souls for Christ and then helping them become reapers also.

This is not to minimize the work of any disciple of Jesus, nor to relegate him to second-class citizenship. The finances of the church must be kept in order. Records must be maintained so we can properly evaluate the church's ministry. Sunday school teachers are an absolute necessity. Other workers in the church do carry out their responsibilities faithfully. The value of the work of those who teach, serve on boards and committees, and do a myriad other jobs in the church is without question. But our discussion here concerns the particular type of worker mentioned by Jesus (Matt. 9:37)—the man or woman who is a fervent witness for Christ and a wise masterbuilder in the lives of others—and we will be using the term in that way.

Characteristics of Potential Workers

Those who are called to this ministry of making disciples need further training to equip them for the ministry that Christ has called them to and placed on their hearts. They have seen the vision for multiplication and are eager to be involved in it. They have a heart for people and are eager to give their lives to helping them. The training they need is in the area of "know-how."

A vision for multiplication. Without a real vision of the power of multiplication, a man will not stick with another person through thick and thin. But when he can look into the face of this other person and see in it the whole world and the potential of reaching it for Christ, his enthusiasm is fired up by the Spirit of God who keeps him motivated and dynamically alive. He joins Paul in stating his goal in life:

> So, naturally, we proclaim Christ! We warn every-one we meet, and we teach everyone we can, all that we know about him, so that, if possible, we may bring every man up to his full maturity in Christ. This is what I am working at all the time, with all the strength that God gives me (Col. 1:28-29, *Phillips*).

Dr. Jerry White, at one time an instructor in the field of astronautics at the United States Air Force Academy, ran an experiment on the school's computer. If a piece of thin india paper, the thickness of a page in the Bible, were folded fifty times, how thick would it be? The computer gave a startling answer—it would stand 17 million miles high. To put that into some kind of understandable perspective, we must remember that the moon is some 239,000 miles away.

This experiment illustrates the tremendous power of multiplication. (What would you rather have, a million dollars a day for thirty days or a penny doubled each day for thirty days?) Multiplication is also possible in the spiritual realm, as Paul expressed to Timothy, "And the things you have heard me say in the presence of many witnesses entrust to reliable men who will also be qualified to teach others" (2 Tim. 2:2). Paul, Timothy, reliable men, others—that is spiritual multiplication.

This concept is further illustrated by Paul's reminder to the Thessalonians, "You became imitators of us and of the Lord; . . . The Lord's message rang out from you not only in Macedonia and Achaia—your faith in God has become known everywhere" (1 Thess. 1:6,8). It is also demonstrated in Jesus' great high priestly prayer: "My prayer is not for them alone. I pray also for those who will believe in me through their message" (John 17:20). It is inherent in the Great Commission: "Teaching them to obey everything I have commanded you" (Matt. 28:20).

Spiritual multiplication may also be seen in the Old Testament. Isaiah recorded these words of the Lord, "And those from among you will rebuild the ancient ruins; you will raise up the age-old foundations; and you will be called the repairer of the breach, the restorer of the streets in which to dwell" (Isa. 58:12).

When a person has produced a disciple, he has reproduced himself as a disciple. He has become a worker. When a person has raised up a worker, he has both reproduced more disciples and himself as a worker. This spiritual multiplication reproduces both disciples and workers.

A heart for people. In addition to the vision for multiplication, the potential worker must have a heart for people. He must see others in light of their potential for God. Christians not only have a tremendous potential *for* God, they are also precious *to* God. They are His beloved children. He wants to see them develop and mature into responsible citizens in the kingdom of God whose lives please Him and bring Him glory. Unless we see people in that light, we will tend to relegate them to some program that we hope will do the job for us.

But God did not relegate us to a program. He got personally involved with us. "For God who said, 'Let light shine out of darkness,' made his light shine in our hearts to give us the light of the knowledge of the glory of God in the face of Christ" (2 Cor. 4:6). His light shone in our hearts. It became a heart-to-heart matter with Him. Without that kind of concern, our discipling process will be cold and mechanical.

Some years ago my wife and I were called to Michigan because of the serious illness of our older son. He was in the hospital on the brink of death. We flew from Colorado Springs to Denver, where we had to change planes. As we entered the terminal to locate the connecting flight, we met Lorne Sanny, president of The Navigators, the organization with which we were affiliated. We noticed that he had been weeping, and as he greeted us he assured us of his prayers and concern.

That night, as we headed east, it was a great comfort to us to know that Lorne was on his knees at the Throne of Grace on our behalf and would likely remain there through the night. He would continue to pray for us while we were in Michigan.

His was more than just the concern of a president for his staff. His was a heart concern—he *felt* with us and *lived* our crisis with us. But it is the Son of God who left us the greatest example. He entered human flesh and identified with us. "Surely our griefs He Himself bore, and our sorrows He carried" (Isa. 53:4). He came to us on our level. He identified with our problems and needs. He showed His great concern when He cried, "O Jerusalem, Jerusalem, you who kill the prophets and stone those sent to you, how often I have longed to gather your children together, as a hen gathers her chicks under her wings, but you were not willing" (Matt. 23:37).

The writer to the Hebrews captured the thrust of this when he said, "Remember those in prison as if you were their fellow prisoners, and those who are mistreated as if you yourselves were suffering" (Heb. 13:3). And Paul reminded the church at Rome:

> Be joyful in hope, patient in affliction, faithful in prayer. Share with God's people who are in need. Practice hospitality.
> Bless those who persecute you; bless and do not curse. Rejoice with those who rejoice; mourn with those who mourn. Live in harmony with one another. Don't be

proud, but be willing to associate with people of low position. Don't be conceited (Rom. 12:12-16).

A heart for people and a vision of the potential of the individual and the power of multiplication are foundational in the life of a worker for Christ.

The Principle of Involvement

Without know-how the disciple with a vision will be frustrated. He will want to do something and become involved with people, but he will be limited in what he can do because he has not had the training he needs to carry his vision out. At this point you can step in and bring both joy to his heart and a contribution to the cause of Christ. You can increase Christ's "harvest workers" by helping him develop into a multiplying disciple. He can take his place on your disciplemaking team and in concert with others on your team broaden your sphere of influence in reaching and helping others.

Involvement, however, is a two-way street. Naturally you are eager to have people become involved with you in your ministry of making disciples. But there is a catch, a hidden factor. To have people become involved with you, you must first become involved with them. This is following God's pattern, for He took the initiative with us, "He has come and has redeemed his people" (Luke 1:69). James reminded the Jerusalem council, "Simon has described to us how God at first showed his concern by taking from the Gentiles a people for himself" (Acts 15:14). And John stated, "This is love: not that we loved God, but that he loved us and sent his Son as an atoning sacrifice for our sins . . . . We love because he first loved us" (1 John 4:10,19).

Jesus came into the world to become involved with His people. And in His involvement with the disciples, He trained them. The principle, then, is this: where there is no involvement, there is no real training. In order to meet the needs of the person whom we are training, we have to know that person and be involved with him.

What to Look for in a Potential Worker

At this stage of your involvement with a person you are well beyond what can be accomplished in a group situation and by passing out general spiritual health tips. Because the element of time now becomes important, you cannot afford to deal in anything except that which meets specific needs and accomplishes specific goals.

Since you only have twenty-four hours in a day and since you only have one life to live, you cannot afford to waste time. This means that you must make sure that the people to whom you give your life are the right ones, those who are ready, eager, and able to assimilate what you have to share with them. And you must make sure that what you teach them actually meets their needs.

It is interesting to watch the mother of a large family, who is on a limited budget, shop in the supermarket. She has learned which are the best buys. She is not taken in by fancy labels or advertising gimmicks. She gets the most for her money. She can spot the best deals out of dozens that might be available. The canned goods she selects go the farthest and provide the most nourishment.

The key to building a road that will do its job is selecting the right materials. That which would do the job in Alaska would not be the best in Malaysia. Climatic conditions call for different building materials. Selection is important.

Selection is also one of the keys to a ministry of making disciples. Jesus taught that principle clearly in His selection of the apostles. Many disciples were following Him; we know of at least seventy in one instance (see Luke 10:1). But out of all these He selected the Twelve for special training. They were first to follow Him, then be involved in the ministry. "'Come, follow me,' Jesus said, 'and I will make you fishers of men'" (Matt. 4:19).

Jesus' selection was made on two bases: personal observation and protracted prayer. He did not rush it, but watched the disciples in the various situations in which they ministered together. Paul would later warn, "Lay hands suddenly on no man" (1 Tim. 5:22, KJV). It takes time to select the right persons with whom to be involved and whom to train.

What do you look for in selecting workers for a discipling team? I believe the primary quality is spelled out for us in Isaiah 58:10: "And if you give yourself to the hungry, And satisfy the desire of the afflicted, Then your light will rise in darkness, And your gloom will become like midday" (NASB). The answer is in one word: *hunger*. They must have a hunger to become makers of disciples, and this hunger may be seen in three areas.

A hunger to be involved in a disciple-making ministry. To pour out your soul is to give your life. That's costly for you and requires a great deal of capacity on a team member's part. If you try to share your life with a person who is not ready, it will drive him off. It will be too much, too soon. Remember that you can make a baby sick quicker by overfeeding than by underfeeding. So look for a person who is eager to be involved in the ministry. This hunger generally takes the form of being available. When you need him, he's there. If you want to get together before breakfast and set the time for 6 A.M., he's there at 5:45 and eager to get started.

In my own experience, one of the men who demonstrated this trait most convincingly was Warren George. He had received some help in a Navigator ministry in Texas, and God had begun to give him a hunger to learn more and to become involved. On a trip through Texas I met Warren, and he asked me if he could come to Omaha and get involved with our team of workers there.

I told him, "Sure, you can come to Omaha if you'd like. We have a Bible study you can get into and occasional rallies you can attend."

He came to Omaha and moved into a room about six blocks from our home. He attended every Bible study that was open to him, and came to all the rallies. He showed great eagerness.

One day I saw that he had moved to a room across the street from us and would gaze out his window at us when our team met in its various functions. It seemed every time I opened the front door, there he was hanging on the screen. He asked if there was anything he could do to help, so I told him he could shovel the snow off our walks and keep the furnace room clean.

That winter we had a tremendous amount of snow, but none of it hit our sidewalks. Warren was out there greeting each snowflake with his shovel. And the furnace room was immaculate. After observing him in these mundane, everyday situations, and after protracted prayer, I invited him to join our team of workers for training. He proved to be faithful and today is responsible for a disciple-making ministry that has hundreds of men and women involved in one of the most productive outreaches for Christ in America.

A hunger for God. In addition to a hunger to be involved, look for the man to have a hunger for God Himself. He should have a strong vertical pull on his life. He should be like the psalmist of old, whose hunger for God was expressed this way, "As the deer pants for the water brooks, so my soul pants for Thee, O God" (Ps. 42:1). David said, "My soul followeth hard after Thee; Thy right hand upholdeth me" (Ps. 63:8, KJV).

A hunger to pay any price. He must know the cost and be willing to pay it. Here you must spell it out and challenge him as Jesus did. "If anyone would come after me, he must deny himself and take up his cross daily and follow me" (Luke 9:23).

I've always had the conviction that if we lay down the challenge to discipleship, committed men will rise to the challenge. That's what Jesus did. After He had spoken some "hard sayings," some of His disciples decided they didn't want to go any further with Him. "From this time many of his disciples turned back and no longer followed him" (John 6:66).

When Jesus saw them leave, He turned to the Twelve and asked, "Do you want to leave too?" (John 6:67). It is interesting that He did not try to intimidate them, plead with them, or coax them to stay. Apparently He was willing to let them walk away if they wanted to do that. But they knew they were not doing Jesus a favor by sticking around; they knew it was for their own benefit that they followed Him, so they stayed. They were willing to pay the price.

I remember a young man who had been showing genuine promise, so I began to discuss the disciple-making ministry with him. His attitude was, "OK, I guess I could give you a little time to help you out in this thing."

One of the first things I had to do was show him that this was not the way it worked. I spelled out to him what was involved, what it would cost in time and energy, what the pressures were, and that there would be times when we would come early and stay late and work harder longer. I tried to communicate to him just what it meant to give your life to people. He liked what he heard, and he's been at it ever since.

This kind of person knows his money, time, and life are not his own. Jesus said, "In the same way, any of you who does not give up everything he has cannot be my disciple" (Luke 14:33).

If this person has these hungers—to be involved, for God Himself, to pay any price—he is ready to become a worker for Jesus Christ.

What to Focus on in Training a Worker

In your ministry with a disciple on a personal, one-to-one level, you must focus on four things: conviction, perspective, excellence, and building depth in his character.

Conviction. Up to this time the potential worker has had your convictions. He has learned why you memorize the Word, study the Bible, and pray, but that will not last him over the long haul. He needs convictions of his own.

Convictions are built in two ways: his own study of the Scriptures and answering "why" questions. A friend of mine went overseas as a missionary and began to develop a disciple-making ministry. Soon some of the Christians in the country where he was serving came to him with a complaint. They felt that some of the things he was emphasizing were "American ideas." They were not convinced they were for their culture. They thought he was trying to impose purely American concepts on them and they resented it.

Wisely my friend pulled back and suggested they study the Scriptures for themselves to see if the ideas were biblical or American. So they all got their Bibles and went to work. They studied many subjects, such as servanthood, the Word, faithfulness, giving, commitment, discipleship. They looked up and carefully examined scores of passages that bore directly and indirectly on each of these subjects.

It took months, but it was well worth the time invested. I have visited this country on a number of occasions and have never met a more disciplined, committed, and convinced band of men and women. They came to their convictions through a study of the Scriptures, and now the ministry has spread and multiplied. At last report, the major problem they faced was finding a facility large enough to hold their rallies.

On another occasion I was working with a group of people who were having a difficult time seeing the importance of the Word of God in their daily lives. I suggested we do a study on Psalm 119. Nothing deep or exhaustive, just reading through the psalm and noting the various verbs that were used in it. Later we read through the psalm again to find the different words that were used in reference to the Word of God. The third time through we tried to catch the psalmist's attitude toward God's Word. It took quite a while, but they came out of the study with some convictions about its importance from God Himself.

The second way of developing convictions is to have the person jot down all the reasons *why* he should be doing these things. Why have a quiet time? Why pray? Why study the Bible? This can be a real eye-opener. Once he has thought through these things, he no longer sails along on what you have told him. He now has a set of convictions of his own. Convictions are deeper than just personal beliefs. He holds his beliefs, but his convictions hold him.

As a practical exercise, have the potential worker review the training objectives given in Chapter 6 and Appendix 1. Ask him to list each one and write out *why* he should be doing it and why it should be part of his life. In case of the negative objectives, ask him to write out why he should avoid them. This may sound a bit tedious, but the potential worker must develop his own convictions on these things if he is to continue in a lifetime of discipleship and making disciples.

Perspective. The second thing you must focus on in training a worker is perspective. When a person comes to Christ, he still remains pretty much a self-centered individual. As he begins growing in the Lord, he gets his sights raised a bit. He begins to be aware of the needs of others in the Sunday school class or in the church fellowship. Then a missionary comes to his church and he is made aware of some different needs; he begins to see the world from a different perspective.

His vision is enlarged. His concerns begin reaching beyond himself. He lives his life on a different plane. He is developing a new perspective. This does not come easily. But at this stage in his life he should be to the point where self is fading into the background and the focal point of his vision is the Lord Himself, the will of God, the work of God, and the needs of others.

Excellence. A third thing a worker should have is a spirit of excellence. He must become proficient in his ministry to others and do it well. His witness, his service, his involvement should reflect the testimony of Jesus Himself, who "has done everything well" (Mark 7:37).

At the International Congress on World Evangelization in Lausanne, Switzerland, in 1974 I met the director of the Toronto Institute of Linguistics. A couple of friends of mine had gone to this excellent school in preparation for service as missionaries. I asked him how they were doing.

He freely admitted that they were not the highest in their class academically, "But," he said, "they are going to come out at the top because they will not permit themselves to settle for less than the best they can do."

"And," he continued, "the motivation seems to come from Jesus Christ Himself."

My friends were committed to excellence. One writer of Scripture prayed:

> May the God of peace, who through the blood of the eternal covenant brought back from the dead our Lord Jesus, that great Shepherd of the sheep, equip you with everything good for doing his will, and may he work in us what is pleasing to him, through Jesus Christ, to whom be glory for ever and ever. Amen. (Heb. 13:20-21).

If we are to be equipped with everything good to do God's will, it must be through Jesus Christ. After all, He is the only one who has ever done all things well. So if you would develop a spirit of excellence in those whom you are training, you must bring them to the place where they turn themselves over to Jesus and let Him live His life through them.

Take the training objectives in Chapter 6 and Appendix 1 and use them again as a practical exercise. This time ask the person whom you are training to go through the list and write out how he can be doing these things in a spirit of excellence. Also have him become so proficient in them that he can share them with another person, one whom he is helping along in his Christian life.

This may seem to be hard work, and it is. But if we are to help a person become an effective worker in the kingdom of God, he must have the whats and whys of discipleship firmly in his mind and heart. And he must be skillful in the ministry of helping others build them into their lives. Superficial, slipshod training and learning will not produce the quality of worker who performs with the standard of excellence reflected in the earthly ministry of Jesus Christ.

Depth of character. The last focus is a continued emphasis on depth in the worker's walk with God and a deepening of his Christian character. Paul stated, "For the kingdom of God consists of and is based on not talk but power—moral power and excellence of soul" (1 Cor. 4:20, *Amplified*).

This is a lifelong emphasis. Faith, purity of life, honesty, humility, and other virtues are never mastered in this life. We continue to grow and mature. This is why John said:

> How great is the love the Father has lavished on us,
> that we should be called children of God! And that is what
> we are! The reason the world does not know us is that it
> did not know him. Dear friends, now we are children of
> God, and what we will be has not yet been made known.
> But we know that when he appears, we shall be like him,
> for we shall see him as he is. Everyone who has this hope
> in him purifies himself, just as he is pure (1 John 3:1-3).

Jesus said that the "harvest is plentiful but the workers are few" (Matt. 9:37; Luke 10:2). The harvest is made up of the harassed and helpless (see Matt. 9:36). This is a picture of a herd of sheep who are totally at the end of their ropes. They are hot, panting, thirsty, tired, and hungry. They are completely helpless and are looking to the shepherd to bring them water and food. They are without hope unless the shepherd aids them.

Paul also described the harvest as being composed of people who were separated from Jesus Christ—excluded, foreigners, without hope, and without God (Eph. 2:11,12). The harvest is obviously plentiful for Paul's words describe the condition of men all around us. The harvest is everywhere and in large numbers. Jesus said the harvest is ready *now* (John 4:35). Obviously the problem is not with the harvest; the problem is with the lack of workers.

Now, a worker is a disciple plus something. In the Scriptures he is described as a worker in the field, one who is harvesting. He is sowing and reaping (John 4:37,38). He is planting and watering (1 Cor. 3:7-9). He is laying the foundation and someone else is building on it (1 Cor. 3:10). He is making disciples (Matt. 28:19,20). A worker is involved in winning the lost and building up the believers—that is, evangelizing and establishing.

Workers help fulfill the Great Commission. Jesus said this is where the need is. We must focus on raising up workers.

CHAPTER 8

HOW TO DEVELOP WORKERS

"Whatever you have learned or received or heard from me, or seen in me—put into practice" (Phil. 4:9).

In late 1971, Lorne Sanny, president of The Navigators, asked me to form a team of men and women to represent our organization at Campus Crusade's "Explo '72" in Dallas, Texas. We designed a display booth and prepared some materials to give away to interested people. We also obtained a British Broadcasting Company film that told the story of the conversion of James Fox, a rising, talented, and popular British motion picture actor.

I had written to James and asked if he could prepare a trailer to tack on to the end of the film that would explain the follow-up he had received after he had come to Christ. He was growing in his Christian life and was well on his way to becoming a fruitful, mature, and committed disciple of Christ. I wanted to show the film and the trailer to the delegates at "Explo '72" to paint a real-life picture of what goes into the discipling ministry.

James wrote back to say that BBC had agreed to shoot it, and that we would have it in time. We received the film right on schedule, and after viewing it I wrote a note of thanks to James. Here is the letter I received in return:

Dear LeRoy:

Thank you for your letter stating that you had received the film and were happy with it.

I would like to relate an incident connected with the

making of the trailer that demonstrates the kind of walk and sense of purpose in fulfilling their ministry that Doug and Leila have [Doug Sparks was the Navigator director for Europe, the Middle East, and Africa, and his wife, Leila, was ill with cancer at the time].

As Doug met me the night before at the station, he told me that Leila and he had been to the doctor and that the growth had been analyzed and was malignant. The following day Doug prepared the script with Chuck and myself. I saw Leila, who spoke of her interest in what I was doing and in the film. Then she cared for the whole family all day as usual.

The following day there were five of us making the film and Doug spent the whole day helping me by holding up cards on which the script was written. Leila saw to it that the crew had all they required.

But as I left the house that night, I thought, what a lot it costs to be in this ministry, where they had both been giving themselves to this film and to those who were making it, at a time when naturally their hearts might have longed to be alone with the Lord and with each other.

When I visited the home, on a trip to London, three weeks ago, Doug was in Finland, but Leila spent 45 minutes encouraging me and teaching her children to have a real interest in what other people are doing.

I believe I have seen a living example of Philippians 2:3-4 and so have been brought closer to the Lord.

Yours in Him,

James Fox

Two prime means of developing a worker for the cause of Christ, one who will be a maker of disciples and an effective and productive member of your disciple-making team, are transmission by example and spending "man-to-man," personal time with him.

Transmission by Example

The letter from James Fox clearly illustrates what transmission by example is all about. The Spirit of God could have used Doug Sparks in a number of ways to get Philippians 2:3,4 into the life of James Fox. That passage states, "Do nothing out of selfish ambition or vain conceit, but in humility consider others better than yourselves. Each of you should look not only to your own interests, but also to the interests of others."

Doug could have met James at the railroad station and the two of them could have discussed that passage. Doug could have said, "All right, James, let's do a little study on this passage. Open your Bible and tell me in your own words what Philippians 2:1-4 says."

James would have done it.

"Very good. Now how about Philippians 2:5-8?"

James might list two or three.

"Fine. Now try to state again in your own words what these verses say to you."

James would do so.

"OK, now let's talk a moment about application. What do you see in these verses that needs expression in your own life?"

In other words, Doug could have led James in a verse analysis study of that passage, and James would have caught something of what Paul was teaching. But that's not what happened. Doug was not even thinking of this passage; he was living it. He was transmitting its truths by his life. The Holy Spirit was infusing that passage into the heart and life of James Fox as he watched the lives of Doug and Leila Sparks. They were not trying to *teach* Philippians 2:3-4; they *were* Philippians 2:3-4. (Leila Sparks died in June 1972, shortly after I received James's letter.)

Paul was an example to the Thessalonians. "Our gospel came to you not simply with words, but also with power, with the Holy Spirit and with deep conviction. You know how we lived among you for your sake" (1 Thess. 1:5). He also wrote to Philemon, "I pray that you may be active in sharing your faith, so that you will have a full understanding of every good thing we have in Christ" (Philem. 6).

Think of what the apostles must have learned about their own racial prejudices when they observed Jesus with the woman of Samaria (see John 4). Think of what they must have learned about concern for the needy as they saw Jesus minister to the sinners, the blind, and the lepers. Think of what they must have learned about dedication and faithfulness as they saw Jesus "resolutely set out for Jerusalem" (Luke 9:51) to go to the cross to die for the sins of men.

Jesus' message was personalized in the everyday affairs of life. His classrooms were the events of the day. He was what He taught. He transmitted His message by His life. For your life to transmit effectively, two things are required: availability and transparency.

Availability. Availability is a two-way street. You cannot train people who are not available, and by the same token, you cannot carry on a meaningful training program if you limit yourself to the formality of the classroom. Jesus and His men were immersed in life together.

John, in reflecting on that incredible experience, spoke of Jesus as the one whom the apostles had looked at and their hands had touched (see 1 John 1:1). You cannot allow yourself to fall into the cuckoo clock routine where, at the appointed hour, you pop out of hiding and speak your piece and then disappear back into seclusion till it is time for another appearance.

If your objective is to impart to your worker some intellectual, theological, or philosophical idea for his consideration, it might work. But if you are out to communicate clearly the insights God has given you on discipleship and making disciples so that he might become a spiritually qualified worker, then it will not work. You must be available to your potential worker constantly. You must be deep in your own fellowship with Jesus Christ so that your life might be a focal point for the energizing power of the Holy Spirit to use as a means of being an example to him.

Transparency. The second quality for effective transmission by example is transparency. Cecil and Thelma Davidson are two of the most effective makers of disciples I have ever met. Their lives are open books. Their home has an open door. Their dinner table has been a meeting place for hundreds of young men and women through the years. These men and women who today are carrying on their own discipling ministry around the world consider themselves part of the Davidson family.

We should exercise great caution in being transparent with others. It may be dangerous to take off our masks, demolish the barriers, and tear down the walls. People then see us as we are, and often some are disappointed. They expected us to be some combination of St. Theresa and John Calvin, but there we stand, ordinary sinners saved by grace. Still, disciples can learn from our mistakes and failures as well as from our successes.

Too much transparency too soon in the development of a new worker may cause harm. Jesus knew that and so told His disciples, "I have much more to say to you, more than you can now bear" (John 16:12). On another occasion earlier in His ministry it was recorded of Him, "With many similar parables Jesus spoke the Word to them, as much as they could understand" (Mark 4:33).

So open your life to those who can handle what they see. Share your heart with that inner core as Jesus did. Often the seventy and even the Twelve were not exposed to certain events in the life of Jesus. "After six days Jesus took with him Peter, James, and John the brother of James, and led them up a high mountain by themselves. There he was transfigured before them. His face shown like the sun, and his clothes became as white as the light" (Matt. 17:1-2).

He shared His heart with the same three at Gethsemane.

> Then Jesus went with his disciples to a place called Gethsemane, and he said to them, "Sit here while I go over there and pray." He took Peter and the two sons of Zebedee along with him, and he began to be sorrowful and troubled. Then he said to them, "My soul is overwhelmed with sorrow to the point of death. Stay here and keep watch with me (Matt. 26:36-38).

Nevertheless, the fact remains that no one can really know you unless you open yourself to him. So we need balance in being transparent with others. I saw this demonstrated at a missionary convention sponsored by Inter-Varsity Christian Fellowship at Urbana, Illinois. A missionary spoke to us and freely admitted his inability to accomplish some of the goals he had set for himself years earlier. He openly confessed his lack of answers for some of the major problems facing his field in the nation where he served. He spoke candidly of his failures as well as his successes.

He contrasted vividly with another man on the program who seemed to be standing on a high ivory pedestal, talking down to us from the vantage point of perfection. The first man seemed to be down there with us, slogging along the same difficult path in which many of us found ourselves, and we identified with him.

At first, being transparent may take the form of sharing with the new worker some of the things you have experienced in your fellowship with the Lord. It may involve your sharing with him some of the victories and defeats, successes and struggles involved in Scripture memory. As you become more involved in the life of this potential worker and he in yours, you will be able to share deeper things, such as the temptations you face, how you handle them, and your battles with the world, the flesh, and the devil.

It is difficult, if not impossible, to be effective in the life of a potential worker unless you are transparent with him. Spiritually qualified workers emerge from the life and ministry of a transparent trainer. Dawson Trotman used to share with us a poem by Edgar Guest that bears on this:

> I'd rather see a sermon
> Than hear one any day.
> I'd rather one would walk with me
> Than merely tell the way.

Training on a Personal Basis

The second prime means of developing a team of workers is to give each person individual and personal attention. It means meeting with each one on a man-to-man basis and having clearly in mind what your training objectives are for *that* person. A ministry of multiplication does not come from an attempt to mass produce disciples. There must be individual, personal time with each person with whom you are working and whom you are training. If you want others to disciple individually, you must work with your potential workers in the same way.

This brings us to some important questions. What do you do in these one-on-one sessions? How often should you have them? Where should you meet?

Where? Anywhere that is convenient. A friend of mine meets the man with whom he is working for lunch in his car in the parking lot near where the man works. Each takes a sack lunch and they meet once a week. What do they do? They share with one another what God has been showing them in their quiet times. They spend some time in the Word together. They usually check each other out on their newly memorized Scriptures. They discuss the ministry God has given them. The man is usually full of questions regarding the ministry of discipleship in the lives of people with whom he is working. Then they pray together.

No hard and fast rule dictates how their time is spent. Occasionally they will spend most of their time praying. On other occasions, the man will bring along a friend from the office to whom he has been witnessing. The three of them meet at a restaurant and the trainer helps his friend in evangelism. He gives his testimony and shares the gospel with the non-Christian. So they accomplish two things: they present the gospel, and the trainee learns something in the process.

The willingness to invest time with a few implies an unwillingness to allow yourself to be spread too thin. Paul spoke of pressing toward the mark and of finishing the course (see Phil. 3:13-14; 2 Tim. 4:7), just as Jesus had finished the work the Father had given him to do (see John 17:4).

A commitment to working with a few people will mean a single-minded approach to life and the ability to sidestep many opportunities that might present themselves. You *could* do many things, but there is one thing you must do if you are to be used of God to fulfill this ministry: you must *concentrate* on a few.

Once you have determined this to be your course, you will have to learn how to say "no" graciously. If God has given you the vision for a ministry in depth, it does not necessarily mean that you will have no ministry in breadth. In fact, if your potential workers become men and women who can effectively lead and meet the needs of others, your ministry will multiply much faster than you could do it yourself. So perseverance and patience are cardinal virtues in the life of the trainer.

Does this mean that you cannot have a public ministry? That someone else will preach all your sermons? That you will have to turn down all invitations to speak at special meetings and conferences? Of course not. Did Jesus have a public ministry? Yes, and quite a broad one at that. He preached in houses, synagogues, on the hillside, at the seaside (Mark 2:1; 3:1; 4:1; Matt. 5:1). He included His example of preaching in the training of the Twelve. He said, "Let's go somewhere else—to the nearby villages—so I can preach there also. That is why I have come" (Mark 1:38).

You must discipline yourself to think in terms of training, to look on the various facets of your ministry as opportunities to build in depth into the lives of your potential workers. This will enable you to keep your priorities straight, and you will be able to gauge what you do by how it contributes to your prime objective of developing spiritually qualified workers. Your ministry will have meaning only as it contributes to the maturing of these men.

What was the ministry of the apostle Paul? Evangelist, theologian, missionary strategist, church planter, teacher, and apostle. But always there were a few key men around him. On one occasion, "he was accompanied by Sopater son of Pyrrhus from Berea, Aristarchus and Secundus from Thessalonica, Gaius from Derbe, Timothy also, and from the province of Asia Tychicus and Trophimus" (Acts 20:4). He used his broad ministry to concentrate on a few.

In writing to the Corinthians, Paul reminded them that he was their spiritual father and challenged them to imitate him. He then informed them that he was sending Timothy to minister to them (see 1 Cor. 4:15-17). Now the question is, If Paul wanted them to imitate *him*, what good would it do to send Timothy? As we read Paul's explanation for sending Timothy, we discover a startling truth. When Timothy came to Corinth, it would be exactly the same as though Paul had come to them. Timothy was more than just an "instructor"; he was actually an extension of the life and ministry of Paul.

Paul could do that because he had confidence in the men he had trained. He later told the Philippians:

> I hope in the Lord Jesus to send Timothy to you soon, that I also may be cheered when I receive news about you. I have no one else like him, who takes a genuine interest in your welfare. For everyone looks out for his own interests, not those of Jesus Christ. But you know that Timothy has proved himself, because as a son with his father he has served with me in the work of the gospel. I

hope, therefore, to send him as soon as I see how things go with me (Phil. 2:19-23).

Likeminded, trustworthy, competent men are not made on a production line like automobiles in an assembly plant. They are carefully and prayerfully developed under the loving guidance of a wise trainer who spends much time on his knees praying for them. In an age of nearly instant everything, we must discipline ourselves to think in terms of quality.

It takes time. It takes effort. It means times of joy and times of tears. It means your life. "This is how we know what love is: Jesus Christ laid down his life for us. And we ought to lay down our lives for our brothers" (1 John 3:16).

Dealing with Some Problems

In working with men in this sort of personal and intensive way, some problems may develop in the life of the trainer.

A possessive attitude. The trainer is in danger of developing a possessive attitude. This usually manifests itself in his using terms such as "My man," "My team," "My trainees." In the New Testament though Paul and the other apostles felt close to the people to whom they ministered and referred to them at times as their "little children," they were also quick to remind them that they actually belonged to Jesus Christ. They were Christ's men and women, not the apostles' followers. Peter had learned this lesson well. Jesus had told him, "Feed *my* sheep" (John 21:17). Later Peter admonished the elders to "feed the flock *of God*" (1 Peter 5:2, KJV). Not "your flock," but "the flock of God."

This unscriptural possessive attitude can stunt the growth of the people involved if the trainer is hesitant to expose them to other men of God who can have an impact on their lives. He can become concerned that his own ministry might lose some of its luster in the eyes of his men if they see others who are equally gifted, perhaps with strengths and abilities that he does not have. Or he can try to build a protective wall around his men to try to keep them exclusively to himself and his ministry.

Dawson Trotman used to do two things that deeply impressed me. He was always bringing in other men to minister to our needs, and he was always willing to let any of his staff go to work for other organizations on loan or permanently if the

Spirit of God led them to do so. Workers are needed everywhere.

A blindness to weaknesses. Another problem is what I call the "rose-colored glasses" danger. As you see disciples develop, realize how far they have come, and watch their growing effectiveness for Christ, it is easy to become blind to their weaknesses. You begin seeing them through "rose-colored glasses"—"my boy can do no wrong!" So you miss whole areas of need in their lives with which you should deal. Again, exposing them to the influence and scrutiny of other godly men will help you evaluate their strengths and weaknesses objectively.

A reproducing of weaknesses. Jesus in His ministry pointed out another potential problem. "A student is not above his teacher, but everyone who is fully trained will be like his teacher" (Luke 6:40). People with whom we are working pick up our strengths as well as our weaknesses. If I have the exclusive input into a man's life, it can lead to that person picking up my weak points, thereby doing him harm as well as good.

As already suggested, the solution to these three potential problems lies in the areas of cross-training and cross-evaluation. We expose our men deliberately to other trainers of disciples who can broaden their horizons and deepen their lives. These will be men who can spot some of their weak points that you overlook or are unable to see because of your close proximity to them. These outside evaluations can help you have a realistic picture of the progress of your men.

In your training you can expect occasional setbacks. It is interesting to note that setbacks occurred in the lives of even the men in Jesus' inner circle—Peter, James, and John. On one occasion James and John displayed a very hateful and destructive attitude—they wanted to call fire down from heaven to destroy an unreceptive Samaritan village (see Luke 9:51-55). Peter denied his Lord three times (see Luke 22:54-62). In the Garden of Gethsemane the inner three were all asleep while Jesus underwent His agony (see Luke 22:45-46). But His confidence in them was rewarded, for His training had not been in vain. They went on to carry out His ministry in the power of the Holy Spirit.

The harvest truly is plentiful, but the workers—the "harvest workers"—are still few. As you give your life to this ministry of training makers of disciples, pray that God will enable you to be an example, work with your men on an individual basis, and correct any problems that might arise.

CHAPTER 9

TRAINING OBJECTIVES
FOR A WORKER

"It was he who gave some to be apostles, some to be prophets, some to be evangelists, and some to be pastors and teachers, to [equip] God's people for works of service, so that the body of Christ may be built up" (Eph. 4:11-12).

I was on a plane with the crew of a motion picture company, and I began chatting with their makeup artist. They had been filming in the high country around Canyon City, Colorado. Charles Bronson, Clint Walker, Jack Warden, and other actors, cameramen, and crew had been there for about three weeks. The man told me he was responsible for what these actors looked like when they faced the cameras. He had his kit with him, full of the tools of his trade. With these, plus his skill as an artist, he would work on the men early each morning. What the public would see on the screen depended on the expertise of this man.

As we chatted about his work, it occurred to me that developing workers for the kingdom of God is something like that. You have the responsibility under God to prepare these people for their ministry in the lives of others. You are concerned with their spiritual makeup: their dedication, commitment, maturity, vision, ministry skills, and the deepening of their lives in the Lord.

You have seen the Holy Spirit accomplish through you life and through the lives of others on your disciple-making team certain specific objectives that have enabled the person you are helping become a mature, committed, and fruitful disciple (see Chapter 6 and Appendix 1). Since he seems to have the hunger, gifts and calling to go on to a ministry of making disciples, you are now ready to build some other qualities into his life.

You are poised on the brink of high adventure, for you are about to help launch a spiritually qualified worker into a world where the harvest continues to be plentiful and where the needs of people scream out for attention. And the workers are few.

At this point you must concentrate on a number of things that will equip the person you are helping and enable him to become a "harvest worker" for Christ. The objectives discussed in this chapter are the process; the product, or end result, is a worker in the harvest fields of the world. At the end of his training, these qualities should be an integral part of his life.

A Heart for People

You must help the potential worker develop a heart for people. It is so easy to fall into the trap of looking on people as a means to an end, a means of accomplishing an objective or fulfilling a vision.

I have watched missionaries fall into this trap. They arrive on the field and gather some people together who seem to be spiritually hungry and have a potential for the ministry. They never actually say this, but their attitudes convey it clearly: "All right, you lucky people, here I am. I've come here and your troubles are over. I've had thorough training, I know my job, and I have arrived spiritually. I'm here to do a job, not play games. God has laid a vision on my heart and you people are the key to seeing it fulfilled. So I want to get something clear right from the beginning. If you people don't get with it and stay with it, my great vision of seeing disciples raised up and starting to multiply will be thwarted. So let's get down to business. I don't have any time to waste."

How do you suppose a national responds to this approach? He probably says to himself, "This man does not really care about me. I'm not important to him as a person. He has no love for me at all. He merely wants to *use* me, not fellowship with me and help me. He has no heart for me at all."

Now that's deadly, for the ministry is not designed to *use* people but to *help* people. I heard a friend of mine say that the reason he stuck around Skip Gray for discipleship training was because he knew that Skip loved him, was concerned for him as an individual, and had only his best interests at heart. Skip was not out to *use* him, but to help him become a mature, dedicated, productive, and multiplying disciple. This attitude reflects the heart of the apostle Paul when he said, "We were gentle among you, like a mother caring for her little children. We loved you so much that we were delighted to share with you not only the gospel of God but our lives as well, because you had become so dear to us" (1 Thess. 2:7-8).

An Addiction to the Vision of Multiplication

The second thing you must do is help the potential worker become addicted to the vision of multiplication. Not only are people precious in the sight of God, but they have a tremendous potential for God. God wants to multiply our lives and ministries of discipleship. We must help our potential workers see the importance of the individual, his potential for God, and how through him many others can become disciples and workers.

An extraordinary example of this principle is found in the ministry of Paul. "Now when I went to Troas to preach the gospel of Christ and found that the Lord had opened a door for me, I still had no peace of mind, because I did not find my brother Titus there. So I said good-by and went on to Macedonia" (2 Cor. 2:12-13).

Was Paul commissioned by Christ to preach the gospel? Yes, Christ had appeared to him and commissioned him "to open their eyes and turn them from darkness to light, and from the power of Satan to God, so that they may receive forgiveness of sins and a place among those who are sanctified by faith in me" (Acts 26:18).

Did Paul have it on his heart to preach the gospel? Yes, for he told the Corinthians, "Yet when I preach the gospel, I cannot boast, for I am compelled to preach. Woe to me if I do not preach the gospel!" (1 Cor. 9:16).

Had he come to Troas to preach the gospel? Yes. Had the Lord opened the door? Yes, He had. But what did Paul do? He left the open door of opportunity to go and find Titus. He left a city with the door wide open to find one man! Why would he do such a thing? For two reasons. One, Titus had just visited the Christians in Corinth and Paul was eager to know their spiritual condition. Two, he did not know the whereabouts of one of his men and was concerned. Titus was important to him. More important than the entire city of Troas? It appears so.

Paul knew that if something had happened to Titus, his ministry would have suffered a serious setback. To Paul, the man was more important than the masses, because the man multiplied was the key to reaching the masses. If he could help keep Titus going and growing, the work of Christ would move ahead rapidly.

As you study the Scriptures, you discover that God's concern is always for the individual. The multitudes are always there and much on the heart of God, but they seem to be the backdrop on the stage of eternity. Stage center is always the man whom God can use to multiply the ministry. He knows that if there is a Joshua or Gideon or Moses or David or Paul, the multitudes will be reached and receive the instruction and help they need.

A Servant Spirit

The third thing you need to do is help the potential worker develop and deepen his servant spirit. In his becoming a worker for Christ, it is critical that he display this attribute in clear and unmistakable terms. He will have to spend the rest of his life giving himself away. His own "rights" will diminish as he serves others.

This was a prime characteristic of Jesus. "For even the Son of Man did not come to be served, but to serve, and to give his life a ransom for many" (Mark 10:45). And it is a necessary quality in the life of a follower of Christ. God will call on him often to sublimate himself to the service of Christ and to the service of others. His basic attitude will have to be that of John the Baptist, who said of Jesus, "He must become greater; I must become less important" (John 3:30). Two things are needed for a person to be a good servant: desire and training.

An Integral Part of the Disciple-making Team

You must help the potential worker learn to function as part of your disciple-making team. He must see himself as a ship in a convoy, as a plan in formation with others. He must know that his individual actions affect the functioning of the whole. This is one of the most difficult things to learn in the discipling ministry. People are individuals and would rather exercise their rights as individuals. One of the greatest problems a leader has to face is the disinclination of people to pull together toward the accomplishing of a common objective. It takes much persistent prayer and gentle, loving guidance to bring people together in this fashion.

Ingredients of a disciple-making team. What components go toward making up a team in which the individual members work well with one another? Four essentials are needed in the formation and ongoing of a disciple-making team.

1. **Bible study.** Get the man with whom you are working involved in a Bible study that has some teeth in it. You should have reasonable standards, such as each person having his study done on time, being at the meeting every time, and sharing freely with the others. Each member studies the same chapter in the Bible, and prepares his study according to a commonly agreed on plan.

Participants should take a few minutes at the beginning of each study to pair off and quote their new Scripture memory verses to one another. In the discussion, as they share what the Holy Spirit has revealed to them in their study and what He impressed them to apply to their lives, He will begin to fuse them together as a team.

2. **Prayer.** Team members must pray together. Center your prayers on the ministry. Pray for those to whom you have witnessed, but who have not yet responded to Christ. Pray for people on your "prospect list," people to whom you would like to take the gospel. Pray for those who are new Christians and are starting on the path of discipleship. Pray for the needs of the ministry. Pray for continued growth and development in your own lives. Pray that God will raise up spiritually qualified workers from your group to go to the ends of the earth with the

3. **Witness.** Share your faith with others as a team. Natu-

rally each man will be carrying on a personal witness where he works and in his neighborhood—in his own sphere of influence among friends, relatives, and neighbors. But from time to time it is good to go out together, in a calling program in your church or some other united witnessing thrust.

4. **Social and fun times.** A speaker told us at a conference that the highest form of identification is having a good time together. Basketball, volleyball, softball, and other team sports do much to knit hearts together. Work projects around the church, going out together, and social gatherings can all be used by the Lord to accomplish unity and the ability to work together as a team.

Unity in a disciple-making team. The concept of the team is oneness. Not sameness of opinion, but *identity of spirit*. So it is vital that your men be committed to some goal that stirs their blood and excites their spirits. Perhaps something like: "To help fulfill Christ's commission by training multiplying disciples." The goal must be something that each of your men will be willing to give his life to, something important, worthy, and grand—like the Great Commission.

Engaging in some noble enterprise, especially if there is a touch of adventure or sacrifice in it, draws men together. Paul spoke of standing "firm in one spirit, contending as one man for the faith of the gospel" (Phil. 1:27). Identity of purpose, if we are truly committed, leads to identity of spirit. Godly men who have joined together with one purpose draw to themselves spiritual forces unfelt before. They find themselves lifted along by a power and enthusiasm which they know is beyond them. They draw from the springs of God and work under the smile and blessing of the Lord. "Behold," the psalmist wrote, "how good and how pleasant it is for brothers to dwell together in unity" (Ps. 133:1).

The presence of the Spirit of God helps a team press ahead with boldness, hope, and joy. It requires an irrevocable commitment to Christ, to the mission, and to each other. Charles Colson speaks of the commitment certain men had to him after he came to Christ, and the strength it brought him during some of his dark hours.

Our unity is what Jesus prayed for. He asked "that all of them may be one, Father, just as you are in me and I am in you.

May they also be in us so that the world may believe that you have sent me" (John 17:21). Our oneness with Christ brings a oneness with each other and enables us to be the right kind of testimony to the world.

Some years ago I did a verse-by-verse meditation study through the Book of Acts. I was trying to discover the secret of the success of the early church. I was fascinated by such statements as, "Ye have filled Jerusalem with your doctrine," "these that have turned the world upside down," and "all they which dwelt in Asia heard the word of the Lord Jesus, both Jews and Greeks" (Acts 5:28; 17:6; 19:10, KJV).

What caused them to make such an impact on their world? After a lengthy and prayerful study, I concluded that it was due to two things: unity and sacrifice. The inspired record frequently mentioned their being of "one accord," "one mind," "one soul," and having "singleness of heart."

The phrase one accord (KJV) appears thirteen times in the Bible, eleven of them in the Book of Acts. The word love, which appears many times in the Bible, is never found in this book. The reason is that the record is not of the meditations of the apostles, but of their acts. The basic undergirding of love led them to a unity of spirit and they were willing to give all they had—their money, their farms, their possessions, their lives—to get the job done. Sacrifice was a normal way of life.

In the Gospels unity is expressed another way. Jesus said, "Again, I tell you that if two of you on earth agree about anything you ask for, it will be done for you by my Father in heaven" (Matt. 18:19). It is interesting to note that the word translated agree in this passage is the same word from which we get our word symphony. A symphony in music is a harmony of different tones and notes. It is not every musician in the orchestra playing the same note at the same time with the same volume. Nor is it every player sounding whatever he wants to. It is a beautiful blend of notes producing the right sound that is pleasant to hear.

Think of your disciple-making team as a symphony. Each man is an individual, not a plastic statue from the same mold as every other. And each man makes his unique contribution in line with his gifts and calling from God.

The apostle Paul suggested another concept to teach

unity. "Instead, speaking the truth in love, we will in all things grow up into him who is the Head, that is, Christ. From him the whole body, joined and held together by every supporting ligament, grows and builds itself up in love, as each part does its work" (Eph. 4:15-16). Here the picture is that of a body whose parts work together in harmony. The idea is one of interdependence, each member functioning in relationship with every other member. The eye and the ear each make a vital contribution; the hand and the foot do the same. We serve each other; we need each other. We minister in harmony with one another. (See also 1 Cor. 12—14 on this harmony.)

So in the Book of Acts you have a picture of unity, "one accord," in the Gospels you have a symphony, and in the epistles you have the concept presented in terms of the body. All of these illustrate the functions of a disciple-making team.

The ministry is far more effective when it is carried on by a team. There is power in a united effort. Teamwork is one of the keys that unlocks and unleashes the power of God. The Lord delights in blessing a band of united Christians functioning together in love and unity.

The team should be seen in terms of a football team rather than a wrestling team. In wrestling there is individual effort by each man as his teammates cheer him on. In football there must be team effort—all eleven men must work together and follow the signals and the play.

When I served in the Marines in World War II, each man was considered a "self-contained unit." But when we hit the beach, we functioned together. We were not a bunch of individual snipers, but a team. The infantry worked together in fire teams: a point man, automatic weapons man, and the rest of the riflemen. In addition, they were supported by tanks, airplanes, and artillery. We were interdependent in times of battle, for we needed each other. We functioned as a team.

That's the picture of the impact of the early church in the Book of Acts. That's what God wants to do with you and your team today. "All believers were one in heart and mind. No one claimed that any of his possessions was his own, but they shared everything they had. With great power the apostles continued to testify to the resurrection of the Lord Jesus, and much grace was with them all" (Acts 4:32-33).

A Volunteer Spirit

The fifth quality to build in a man's life is a volunteer spirit. This is difficult to do in an age which says, "Never volunteer for anything." But a volunteer spirit is a Christlike spirit. Jesus was not carried to the cross kicking and screaming. He went to Jerusalem knowing what He would face.

> They were on their way up to Jerusalem, with Jesus leading the way, and the disciples were astonished, while those who followed were afraid. Again he took the Twelve aside and told them what was going to happen to him. "We are going up to Jerusalem," he said, "and the Son of Man will be betrayed to the chief priests and teachers of the law. They will condemn him to death and will hand him over to the Gentiles, who will mock him and spit on him, flog him and kill him. Three days later he will rise" (Mark 10:32-34).

He went to Jerusalem as a volunteer. He gave His life of His own free will. "The reason my Father loves me is that I lay down my life—only to take it up again. No one takes it from me, but I lay it down of my own accord. I have authority to lay it down and authority to take it up again. This command I received from my Father" (John 10:17-18).

For a person to be involved in a disciple-making ministry, a volunteer spirit is a must. Half-hearted participants do not make good workers. A classic example of whole-hearted volunteering is in the life of Isaiah: "Then I heard the voice of the Lord, saying, 'Whom shall I send, and who will go for us?' Then I said, 'Here am I. Send me!'" (Isa. 6:8). This is the spirit all of us need.

A Pacesetter

In order to teach others the truths of Christ and the Christian life, the potential worker must live them out in his own life. He must set the pace for those whom he is helping. In order to help others in the disciplines of Christian living, he must be practicing them himself. God does not use someone with a weak, run-down-at-the-heels prayer life to help another develop into a strong man of prayer.

If he would help another person establish a consistent

quiet time, he must be meeting with the Lord on a regular basis. Paul said, "Whatever you have learned or received or heard from me, or seen in me—put it into practice. And the God of peace will be with you" (Phil. 4:9). He told the Corinthians, "Follow my example, as I follow the example of Christ" (1 Cor. 11:1).

It is not the pacesetter's job to outrun everybody. His responsibility is to help the other runners do their best. The pacesetter must instruct and guide, not impress. He is there to help the disciple "run with perseverance the race marked out for us" (Heb. 12:1).

A Productive Witness

You must help the potential worker become a productive witness. It is easy for a person, when he gets to this stage of his spiritual growth and development, to fall into the trap of being a "fellowshiping" Christian rather than one who is continually engaged in the battle for the souls of men. If he stays active in sharing the gospel with others, three things will happen:

1. The ranks of new believers will increase.
2. He will provide an example to other disciples.
3. He will attract into further training those who have a warrior's spirit, a heart for the battle, and a desire to become workers for Jesus Christ.

If he doesn't stay active, he will begin to neglect some vital areas of the Christian life, for it is easy to be drawn away into other "important" things.

My wife and I had an experience that brought this home to us in a forceful way. We were in Lincoln, Nebraska to speak at a week-long conference of the Back to the Bible Broadcast. One of the staff met us at the airport, took us to the apartment in the Broadcast building, got us settled, and pointed out a nearby restaurant where we could have supper.

After he left, Virginia and I walked over to the restaurant. We found ourselves the only customers in the place. I ordered a hamburger for myself and a salad for Virginia, and we waited for our meal. We waited and waited and waited. Eventually a nervous waitress came to our table and said, "Oh, Sir, your food will be here shortly."

"Fine," I said, "we're in no hurry." So she left.

After another long wait she came back. "Oh, Sir," she said, this time wringing her hands, "your food will be here any minute now."

"Fine," I assured her, "we're in no hurry. Don't be nervous."

She scampered away and returned after another long wait. "Oh, Sir," she said, still wringing her hands, "your food will be here in a second."

I smiled. "OK," I said, "I'll time you." And I looked at my watch.

"No, no!" she blurted out. "I don't mean exactly one second—I mean real soon."

I smiled again. "OK," I replied, "we're in no hurry."

She still appeared nervous, so I tried to calm her. "Look," I said, "here am I with the most beautiful girl in the world [my wife]. I'm sitting in this lovely restaurant with my sweetheart. We're enjoying it. There is no reason for us to be in a hurry."

She appeared relieved, but my curiosity had been aroused. "By the way," I said, "not that I'm angry or anxious to get away or anything like that, but why does it take so long to cook my hamburger?"

"Oh, Sir," she said, "the cooks forgot to cook it!"

I was amazed. Forgot to cook it! How could that be? So I said, "Let me ask you—why does this restaurant hire cooks? What are they supposed to do?"

"Cook," she replied.

"I thought so," I said. "Then how could they forget to cook my hamburger if they are hired to cook?"

"Well," she answered, "tomorrow the inspectors are coming, and the cooks are busy getting ready for inspection. They are washing the floors and walls, scrubbing the pots and pans, cleaning the stove, and doing other things to get ready."

I understood. I have seen it happen in the Christian enterprise as well. People can get busy in so many good things that they forget the main objective.

Jesus last words to us are still on record: "But you will receive power when the Holy Spirit comes on you; and you will be my witnesses in Jerusalem, and in all Judea and Samaria, and to the ends of the earth" (Acts 1:8).

A Bible Study Leader

Since much of the work in which your potential worker will be involved can be done in the setting of a small group Bible study, you must help him become an excellent Bible study leader. As he leads the study, he will discover that some of the members will become available to him for some one-on-one time. If he plans his study carefully, prays over it faithfully, and leads it effectively, that small group may produce some disciples and workers.

Two things happened in people's lives when Jesus opened the Scriptures to them: their minds were enlightened and their hearts began to burn.

> They asked each other, "Were not our hearts burning within us while he talked with us on the road and opened the Scriptures to us?" . . . Then he opened their minds so they could understand the Scriptures (Luke 24:32, 45).

In light of that, the potential worker must do his homework, pray, and be ready to lead the group from his own deep and thorough study. He must also share his application—his own heart involvement with the truth. Knowledge alone is not enough. It must be knowledge on fire, the truth of God made alive by the enlightening power of the Holy Spirit. It must be more than just facts, more than just excitement, more than just emotion. It must be a blend of honest, hard work, in which the teaching of the passage is dealt with correctly, and the communication of a holy zeal for the truth of God.

One summer I was involved with a training program for college students at Maranatha Bible Camp near North Platte, Nebraska. Dwight Hill was the leader that summer and I stopped in to see how things were going. I asked one of the staff how Dwight was getting along.

"He's doing great," the man said. "It's really remarkable to see him in action. And you know, when he sits down under a tree with another man and opens his Bible, something happens!"

That's the mark of a good Bible study leader. When he

gets his group together over their open Bibles, something happens. They leave the study enlightened and motivated.

A Sensitivity to Others

The ninth objective is for you to help your man in the area of sensitivity to others. He communicates with others by his speech, his attitude, and his actions—what he says and how he says it, what he does and how he does it. He must learn how to *say* the right thing in the right way at the right time; he must learn how to *do* the right thing in the right way at the right time.

Jesus' sensitivity to others is our prime example. His approach to Zaccheus (see Luke 19:1-10) was different from His approach to the woman at the well (see John 4:2-42). He dealt with Andrew differently than He dealt with Peter (see John 1:35-42). His invitation to the people to follow Him differed on various occasions (compare Matt. 11:28-30 with Luke 9:23-26). He touched each situation with exactly the right word in exactly the right way. There was no "standard approach." He did not blast His way through humanity like a tank. Instead, He had the touch of a master craftsman in forming each life He was involved with into a thing of beauty.

The apostle Paul stated, "So I strive always to keep my conscience clear before God and man" (Acts 24:16). James had some clear words on the use and misuse of the tongue (see James 3).

A sensitivity to the situation will sometimes lead you to say nothing. On other occasions it will cause you to roll up your sleeves and plunge right into the middle of it. God's dealings with His people in slavery in Egypt is an illustration of this point. He knew their sorrows, He heard their cries, but He kept silent for years. Then when His leader was prepared, He moved in with bold and forthright actions. He solved the problem at the right time in the right way.

A sensitivity to the sufferings and needs of people should not be confused with sentimentality. The utter absence of sentimentality in the life of Jesus is what makes His compassion stand out so vividly, At one point in His ministry He was approached by a man who had been cheated by his brother. "Someone in the crowd said to him, 'Teacher, tell my brother to divide the inheritance with me'" (Luke 12:13).

Jesus could have tried to comfort the man with words couched in tender and sentimental phrases. "Oh, you poor man! I feel so sorry for you. So your mean old brother is cheating you? How awful! Well, cheer up. Things may get better. Someday there will be 'pie in the sky' and all will be well." But He didn't.

His answer was classic. It was full of genuine compassion, not the lukewarm slush of sentimentality. "Man, who appointed me a judge or an arbiter between you? . . . Watch out! Be on your guard against all kinds of greed; a man's life does not consist in the abundance of his possessions" (Luke 12:14-15).

His objective was to help these men. Their problem was covetousness. So He turned to both of them and tried to lift them above their present level of wallowing in the mire of a covetous spirit. One had the money; the other wanted it. Jesus tried to raise both of them to a higher plane.

Words can sting; they can wound; they can heal. A wise man will know how to give and take reproof. "Do not reprove a scoffer, lest he hate you; reprove a wise man, and he will love you. Give instruction to a wise man, and he will be still wiser; teach a righteous man, and he will increase his learning" (Prov. 9:8-9).

Solomon also said, "A man has joy in an apt answer, and how delightful is a timely word" (Prov. 15:23). "Like apples of gold in settings of silver is a word spoken in right circumstances" (Prov. 25:11).

A Thinker

The last objective you have with your potential worker is to help him to think. A businessman said, "I can get people to do anything except two things: think and do things in the order of their importance."

Paul advised Titus, "These, then, are the things you should teach. Encourage and rebuke with all authority. Do not let anyone despise you" (Titus 2:15). What did Paul mean by the term *despise?* The word comes from a Greek root from which we get our English word *periphery.* The thrust of his injunction to Titus is for the younger man not to let people think mental circles around him and so look down on him as a poor thinker. The best way for a worker to command the respect of those with whom he is involved is to do the kind of thinking that will merit it.

To learn to think is to learn to keep alert, to be observant, and to keep your mind in gear. Dawson Trotman used to try to help us in this area. After we'd leave someone's house, he would remark, "Weren't those beautiful drapes? Did you notice how they blended in with the color of the carpet?" Usually I would stare at him and be forced to admit that I hadn't even noticed that there were drapes and carpet. He tried to help us learn to think by observation.

Solomon was an observant man and a thinker. "I passed by the field of the sluggard and by the vineyard of the man lacking sense; and behold, it was completely overgrown with thistles, its surface was covered with nettles, and its stone wall was broken down. When I saw, I reflected upon it; I looked and received instruction" (Prov. 24:30-32). He looked . . . and learned.

The person who has to have everything spelled out for him will miss many valuable lessons in life. So try to help your men learn to make disciples by being alert to what goes on around them. Help them think through on the consequences of their actions. "If we do this, will that occur? If that occurs, will this take place? If this takes place, is that likely to result? Do we want that result? No? Then let's not start down that road in the first place."

* * *

With these ten training objectives you have worked on things that affect the attitudes, personal life, spiritual development, and ministry skills of your potential worker. As you look over the list, you may want to add some or delete some. They are not intended to be hard and fast rules, but illustrative of the kinds of qualities that are necessary to equip the worker—the "harvest worker."

Earlier we looked at training objectives (Chapter 6 and Appendix 1) that were part of the establishing process that helped your man grow from being a convert to becoming a fruitful, dedicated, mature disciple. These ten objectives are part of the equipping process that results in a committed, knowledgeable, productive worker. Illustrated, it looks like this:

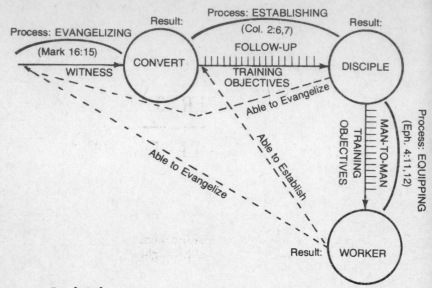

In this diagram we can see the man in perspective. He is now equipped to reach out in evangelism, resulting in converts, and then establish these new Christians to make them disciples.

You may find it valuable to think through on each of these objectives in the same way you did the earlier ones. Make your own check sheet, defining the objective, listing the activities you would use, finding additional materials, and writing down the Scriptures you would share.

CHAPTER 10

THE NEED FOR LEADERSHIP

"He appointed twelve—designating them apostles—that
they might be with him and that he might send them out
to preach" (Mark 3:14).

In order to reproduce a disciple-making ministry, a person who
has become a disciple and has been trained to be a worker must
take one more step. He must become a leader. The last stage in
the development of this person in preparing him for this ministry is leadership.

This is not to say that once these lessons are learned
growth and development will come to a stop. No, for growth is
a lifetime process. We never arrive during our lifetimes.

How great is the love the Father has lavished on us,
that we should be called children of God! And that is what
we are! The reason the world does not know us is that it
did not know him. Dear friends, now we are children of
God, and what we will be has not yet been made known.
But we know that when he appears, we shall be like him,
for we shall see him as he is. Everyone who has this hope
in him purifies himself, just as he is pure (1 John 3:1-3).

You have watched the person take the steps from convert to
disciple. You have seen him go on to become a worker—a
"harvest worker"—one who knew how to make disciples and
was part of your disciple-making team. Now there is one more
step to take. You must look over the men on your team and see
if there are one or two in the group who should be taken
further.

125

Are there those who have the gifts, abilities, and calling of God to become leaders of a disciple-making ministry? Those who could do what you are doing? If so, they will need some special leadership training to do the job.

You must realize and note carefully that we are not talking about whether or not the person is going to become a "full-time" Christian worker, pastor, or missionary. He may, but that's not the issue. Many "laymen" are some of the finest leaders of disciple-making ministries in the world today. They are highly respected by "full-time" Christian workers who know them and are often called on to train pastors and missionaries in this ministry. Their occupation or profession is what they do for a living and they are successful in it. But leading a team of workers is their life.

The two keys to developing a leader of a disciple-making team are selection and time. We want to examine these carefully.

The Importance of Selection

You have been ministering to the potential leader for many months, possibly years. You knew him as a convert. You established him by helping him become a fruitful, committed, and productive disciple. You equipped him by giving him the training he needed to become a worker, a member of your team of disciple makers. Now you are at a critical point in his life. Is God leading him to take the next step, to become a leader of a team of men who are able to make disciples of others?

At least five qualities characterize a leader; you must look for them in a potential leader. All five need not be present in a person's life. He does not have to be a spiritual superman or a saintly superstar, but if two or three of these are evident, you should pray seriously for the leading of the Lord as to your further involvement with him in giving him more leadership training. If you are serving on a mission field where the harvest is very plentiful and the workers are very few, this is especially crucial.

To illustrate the reasoning behind this stage of training, let's say you are a missionary on the island of Java in Indonesia. You have a band of workers serving with you. You know there are millions of people scattered throughout the thousands of islands of the country who need spiritual help. How will they get it?

Possibly you are the key. Perhaps the Lord would lead you to give some of your workers special leadership training to go to these places and do what you are doing. It would be a thrill to watch them go out, reach some people for Christ, stick with those people till they became fruitful, dedicated, mature disciples, and then have some of those go on to become effective workers on their disciple-making teams.

In selecting your leaders for training, these are the five qualities to look for.

He has fight and drive. He does not give up easily. He does not turn and run at the first sign of opposition, nor does he stop at the first obstacle. He presses ahead with enthusiasm, a positive attitude, dedication and faith, regardless of the opposition, distractions, and trials in his involvement in Jesus' Great Commission.

He reflects the response Paul had when the Holy Spirit told him that prison, suffering, and troubles were waiting for him. "However, I consider my life worth nothing to me, if only I may finish the race and complete the task the Lord Jesus has given me—the task of testifying to the gospel of God's grace" (Acts 20:24).

He knows the path will not be easy. He realizes that he who walks the high, hard, windswept path often walks alone. He does not expect to slide toward the mark, or drift or glide or slip or float. He knows there will be opposition. He is perfectly willing to press toward the goal in his high calling from God (see Phil. 3:14). He will gladly knuckle down and fight the good fight of faith.

He accepts the road of suffering: "For it has been granted to you on behalf of Christ not only to believe on him, but also to suffer for him" (Phil. 1:29). Look for that spirit, for the leader must keep going whether others do or not.

He can spot and recruit achievers. This is important because it will determine what kind of team he will begin to form. He must know the difference between a good man and a nice guy. He must be able to spot and recruit good men. Why is that important? If he accumulates a bunch of hangers-on around him, the good men will stay away. The only way they will know what is involved is by what they see.

I was talking to a young medical doctor one time who had this ministry on his heart. He told me he was thinking of giving much time and attention to a certain man. I asked him if that was the type of person he eventually wanted to have on his discipleship team.

"No," he answered, "but he's the only man available right now."

I cautioned him to wait a while to see if God might bring an achiever into his path. God did, and today there are men from that ministry who are leading disciple-making teams in the United States, Canada, Latin America, the Orient, and Australia. Much of the success of his ministry goes back to that initial decision to wait for the right man to come along.

How do you spot an achiever? Here are some traits to look for:

1. **He is reliable.** This doesn't mean he never makes mistakes. Everyone does. But when he is given a job, he will see it through. An Old Testament prophet told a parable of a man who was told to guard a prisoner, but the prisoner escaped. His classic answer was, "While your servant was busy here and there, he was gone!" (1 Kings 20:39-40). His problem was unreliability. They gave the job to the wrong man.

2. **He is resourceful.** He does the best he can with what he's got. Dawson Trotman loved to tell the story of the night the follow-up department ran out of materials in the counseling room of the first Greater London Billy Graham Crusade. One of the counselors came running up to Trotman and said, "We've run out of *Beginning with Christ* packets!"

"That's OK," Trotman replied. "They probably ran out of them on the day of Pentecost when 3,000 were converted."

At first the man looked blank, then puzzled, and finally he saw the point. They didn't have *Beginning with Christ* packets at Pentecost and they managed very well. With a little resourcefulness they could do the same in London. And they did.

Lorne Sanny, president of The Navigators, often preaches to us about Shamgar, who started where he was and did the best he could with what he had. The battle with the Philistines was raging and he had no sword. So he fought the enemy with an ox goad and killed six hundred of them (see Judg. 3:31).

3. **He is adaptable.** Paul spoke of this trait at length to the Corinthians.

> Though I am free and belong to no man, I make myself a slave to everyone, to win as many as possible. To the Jews I became like a Jew, to win the Jews. To those under the law I became like one under the law (though I myself am not under the law), so as to win those under the law. To those not having the law I became like one not having the law (though I am not free from God's law but am under Christ's law), so as to win those not having the law. To the weak I became weak, to win the weak. I have become all things to all men so that by all possible means I might save some. I do all this for the sake of the gospel, that I may share in its blessings (1 Cor. 9:19-23).

Leaders are often called on to do a variety of things. One Sunday I began a series of meetings in Minneapolis. The preceding Saturday, I spoke to a group of youth directors on the subject of discipleship and gave my testimony to about 16,000 young people at a rock festival. And the day before that I spoke to the U. S. leadership of the Christian Business Men's Committee on the subject of making disciples. A leader has to adapt.

The leader must be a specialist and disciple making must be his life. But he must also be versatile. He must have the ability to roll with the punches and fit into various situations. He will be called on to serve all kinds of groups and minister to all kinds of people.

4. **He is enthusiastic.** His heart is in the ministry and he gives it all he's got. He has to have the attitude of the psalmist toward God: "With all my heart I have sought Thee; do not let me wander from Thy commandments" (Ps. 119:10).

This trait is important to have. A man may make some dumb mistakes, but if he is really trying and giving it his best, then he can be forgiven his mistakes. Look for the man who is eager, not just "open." Look for the man who is "hot to go," not just the man who is willing.

I was talking one day to a young man who was leading a team of disciples at the United States Air Force Academy. He wanted to know if I would like his team of men to come over to our house some Saturday and work on the lawn. I thought it sounded like a great idea, so we set a date. About three days before they were to come he called me and said, "Well, LeRoy, I've got six men who are willing to come Saturday."

I said okay and hung up the phone. But his words began to gnaw at me. These men were willing; not eager, but willing. It went against everything I had ever done. I had never purposely allowed myself to get involved in a project with men who were merely willing. I have learned that if a man is just doing something because he feels he has to, he will not do his best. I didn't want half a dozen men working on my lawn whose hearts weren't in it, because they would likely do sloppy work. So I called the leader back and cancelled the project.

5. **He knows how to work.** Jesus did not call the sunbathers on the Sea of Galilee beach who were lying around frying in their own fat. He called the fishermen who were mending their nets. Centuries before, God called Moses while he was tending sheep in the desert, and later David while he was out in the fields working. Christian work is hard work.

We were having a conference at our headquarters and the crowd was so large we had to use a fourth floor room for a workshop. It meant carrying about seventy-five chairs from the truck outside and up four long flights of stairs. One of the men looked at me and said, "Man, this is work!"

"Yes," I told him, "that's how the ministry is often referred to—the Navigator *work*." In running a Navigator conference, we were involved in the work of The Navigators.

So look for the man who is eager to work harder longer. He may have the stuff of which leaders are made.

6. **He is alert.** A leader of "harvest workers" must be alert to what is going on around him. Failure in this area can often hinder his effectiveness in the ministry of making disciples of others.

I was watching a World Series baseball game. The catcher wanted the pitcher to throw an outside curve and just graze the corner of the plate. It required great skill and concentration to throw the ball at just the right height and into that tiny area. At the same time a fast runner was on first base, giving every indication of trying to steal second. Had the pitcher not watched him carefully, he would have done it. But the pitcher was an old pro. He never lost the concentration of his primary objective—to throw a strike to the batter—but he watched the runner as well. He was alert.

The alert person knows where he is going and how to get there. But he is not so restricted in his vision that he is not alert to what is taking place in other areas of life around him. His aim may be narrow, but his vision is broad.

One way you can spot an alert man is through conversation. Is he aware of what is happening around him? Can he look and receive instruction? (see Prov. 24:30-32). The alert man can learn from the world around him. The person who does not have this quality is limited and is among the ranks of the millions who need to be taught everything, step by step.

7. **He has initiative.** I was speaking at a men's retreat in Northern California. The time for the meeting had come, but the leaders had not appeared. One of the men in the front row looked around the room and remarked that it was time for the meeting. He kept glancing at his watch. We were wasting the time of 150 men who had left their families to come to this retreat. After a few more glances around the room, this man stood up, quieted everyone down, and started the meeting. In that instant he became our leader.

Initiative is one of the basic marks of an achiever. He is aware of what needs to be done and takes steps to do it. He does not need to be pushed, for he is a self-starter. Scripture does not indicate that the apostle Peter "planned" to preach his sermon on the day of Pentecost. But when the opportunity came, he was ready in the enabling power of the Holy Spirit. He stood up, took the initiative, and preached. We know the results.

Scripture does not tell us that some time later Peter "planned" to command the lame man at the Beautiful Gate to rise and walk (see Acts 3:1-7). But he was ready, and in the name of Jesus of Nazareth he took the initiative. We know the results. This trait is vital to a leader.

8. **He is confident.** He will have to be with a variety of people and he should be at home with them all. The rich will call him to serve; the poor will need his help. The high and mighty as well as the lowly people of God will need his ministry and call on him to lend a hand.

To be able to serve one group well but run from another is not a Christlike characteristic. Jesus could stand in the presence of the religious leaders in Jerusalem and minister effectively. He could sit in a lowly home in Galilee and do the same. The common people heard Him gladly. He had an effective ministry in the life of Nicodemus, a ruler of the Jews.

The apostles ministered to multitudes in Jerusalem and also were able to reach some priests. Paul could minister to a young, timid man like Timothy, and at the same time have as his friends certain chiefs of the province of Asia.

* * *

These eight marks of an achiever may prove helpful to you as you look over your workers in search of the one who may have the potential to be a leader. Every one of these traits does not have to be in full bloom in the man's life, but be on the alert for some of them, even in the budding stage.

You are not looking for the Hercules of the Christian faith. We all have our strengths and weaknesses. We do some things better than others. This list is merely illustrative of what you might consider important in the area of achievement as you begin to select a man for training in leadership.

He has stability. He can take the pressure. Leadership is full of it—from all sides, from many people, some positive and some negative. Some people will be making constant demands on him to do more. Others, who don't like what he is doing, will fight him.

I was ministering in a city where the pastor of one of the largest churches in town had as his goal to drive a Christian worker and his ministry out of town. He brought all sorts of pressure to bear on the man—false accusations, a whispering campaign. It became almost unbearable, but the man stuck to his guns and followed his call from God. In the midst of tremendous opposition, he had a successful ministry. Many people came to Christ as a result.

The normal pressures of life will press in—financial difficulties, family problems, prolonged sickness. David was a man after God's own heart, yet he had problems—his men spoke of stoning him, his wife turned against him, his son rebelled against him. The pressures were there, but he served God in his generation.

Stability is a necessary quality of a leader and it comes from having a firm belief in the sovereignty of God. To know that God in heaven is in control (see Ps. 115:3); to know that all things do, in fact, work together for good and are brought our way to conform us more and more into the image of Jesus Christ (see Rom. 8:28-29); to know that God's hand is shaping and molding the events of our lives.

Trust is the key to stability. Trust in God as the loving, caring heavenly Father. A little poem says it well:

> Said the Robin to the Sparrow:
> "I would really like to know
> Why these anxious human beings
> Rush about and worry so?"
>
> Said the Sparrow to the Robin:
> "Friend, I think that it must be
> That they have no Heavenly Father
> Such as cares for you and me."[1]

He has organizational ability. He can weld men together into a team. This is a man who knows the simple fact that two men can accomplish more than one if they are properly related to one another and are organized. He knows the same is true of three, four, or more men. A project of any size can be broken down into workable units with proper organization.

One of the real clues to a man's ability to organize others is to see if he's organized himself. Does he set realistic goals for himself? Does he achieve them? Is he prompt or chronically late? Is he an opportunist or a strategist? Does he just seem to do whatever shows up next or does he plan his life in accordance with certain God-given goals and priorities? If he can't organize himself, he certainly will not be able to organize others.

Personal organization is something that can be learned. Six keys to it are:

1. A realistic look at one's own capacity.
2. A settled conviction as to what God wants done.
3. The ability to do things in the order of their importance.
4. The good sense to leave some free time between projects, knowing things often take longer than planned and that there are always unforeseen interruptions.

5. The faithful keeping of time with God and the priority of the family at the top of the list.

6. Learning how to function with a certain flexibility that is people-centered rather than project-centered. No one can be a good leader who is more concerned with projects than with people.

Six basic rules which will help a person organize a project or event are:

1. Define your mission in exact, specific terms.

2. Break it down and divide it up into manageable and workable units.

3. Set up an organization that will help each unit to accomplish its part of the endeavor.

4. Fill the key spots with well-trained men.

5. Give them full authority to get their jobs done.

6. Check up on them to see that they stick with the main job.

In the 1950s, I worked with Don Rosenberger, then the director of the Christian Youth Crusade in Washington, D. C. Here is a poem he shared with me:

Organization

There may be nothing wrong with you,
The way you live, the work you do,
But I can very plainly see
Exactly what is wrong with me.
It isn't that I'm indolent
Or dodging duty by intent;
I work as hard as anyone,
And yet I get so little done.
The morning goes, the noon is here,
Before I know, the night is near,
And all around me, I regret,
Are things I haven't finished yet.
If I could just get organized!
I oftentimes have realized
Not all that matters is the *man;*
The man must also have a plan.

With you, there may be nothing wrong,
But here's my trouble right along;
I do the things that don't amount
To very much, of no account,

That really seem important though
And let a lot of matters go.
I nibble this, I nibble that,
But I never finish what I'm at.
I work as hard as anyone,
And yet I get so little done,
I'd do so much you'd be surprised,
If I could just get organized![2]

He has judgment and creativity. These are placed together because they are interrelated, though with many people one usually dominates. If the judicial mind is predominant, the person will be a steady, thoughtful, methodical, productive leader. If the creative streak is predominant, the person will "get it done with a flair." He will not necessarily be flamboyant, but there will be a bit more sparkle and pizzazz in his method of operation.

The judicial mind, however, is well able to come up with innovative and creative ideas, and it often does. That type of person merely implements these new ideas in a solid, matter-of-fact manner. The creative mind must do two things: have the good sense to discard the ten mediocre ideas that burst into its consciousness and keep the good one, and to implement it just as surely, though often with a bit more excitement.

The most sensible thing each of these types can do is to make sure they have a counterpart on their team. Here is where the variety of gifts and abilities comes into play. It is a mistake for the leader to fill his team with personalities similar to his own, just because he feels more secure with them. He will do well to have some close collaborators that are at the opposite end of the spectrum in personality, gifts, and abilities. This brings balance to the team and a greater flexibility and effectiveness. Jesus certainly practiced this principle.

* * *

These, then, are five qualities to look for in the selection of potential leaders. The leader of a team of workers has a rare and important function in the cause of Christ and should be selected after a great deal of observation and with much prayer.

The Element of Time
The second key to developing a leader of a disciple-making

team is time. You must be willing to spend a great deal of time with the person. The example that was set by Jesus comes through clearly. The example of the apostle Paul is equally obvious. Time must be spent together in the ministry, in your home, in his home, in the normal affairs of life, on trips, at work, and at play.

Time is spent together in the Word discussing doctrine, principles, problems, and blessings. Time should be spent together in prayer and planning. You will want to share your personal battles, your victories and defeats, just as he does with you.

This investment of time, of course, is costly. But if you are called of God to help multiply workers in the harvest fields of the world, you will not be swayed simply because something is tough and costly. And spending time with another person certainly is. Tears, disappointments, thwarted dreams, and heartaches big enough to make you want to give up await you down the line.

Some years ago I was working with two young men who showed great potential. I loved those two men and ached to see them amount to something in the cause of Christ. We spent hours, days, months, and years together. We studied the Bible; we prayed. We traveled to weekend conferences and church retreats. But just when I thought we were making some headway, one or both of them would do something so foolish I couldn't believe it.

I would help pick up the pieces and we would continue. I have no way of calculating the hours I spent in prayer for them. After many years of joy, laughter, bewilderment, disappointment, and victory, they are both carrying a major responsibility in the work of God. They are "harvest workers" in every sense of the term. But it took a great deal of time.

The apostle Paul is a classic example of a leader who spent time with men to help train them for leadership. Timothy accompanied Paul on his journeys. "But you know that Timothy has proved himself, because as a son with his father he has served with me in the work of the gospel. I hope, therefore, to send him as soon as I see how things go with me" (Phil. 2:22-23).

Because of their close association, Paul could say, "You,

however, know all about my teaching, my way of life, my purpose, faith, patience, love, endurance, persecutions, sufferings—what kinds of things happened to me in Antioch, Iconium and Lystra, the persecutions I endured. Yet the Lord rescued me from all of them" (2 Tim. 3:10-11).

Disappointments came to Paul, for some of the men he had spent time with turned their backs on him. "Demas, because he loved this world, has deserted me and has gone to Thessalonica" (2 Tim. 4:10).

The Lord Jesus is the best example of one who invested much time in the lives of a few men. "He ordained twelve, that they should be with him, and that he might send them forth to preach" (Mark 3:14, KJV). The majority of His time was spent with the Twelve.

Spending time with a person is an important aspect of leadership training. It is scriptural. Also, a person whom you see only periodically can fake it while he is with you. But given the time frame we see in the leadership training carried on by Jesus and Paul, there is no way that the men could have put on an act. Jesus knew His men well, including Judas.

Selection is important because you would not want to invest all that time of training a leader only to discover you have gone through it all and done it all with the wrong man. Time is important because it takes time to do a right job. Some may think, *I don't have that kind of time. Surely there must be a quicker way.* But there isn't. The time-tested methods of Jesus are still applicable today.

Notes

[1]Elizabeth Cheney, quoted by Mrs. Charles E. Cowman, *Streams in the Desert* (Grand Rapids: Zondervan Publishing House), October 10, p. 294.
[2]Source unknown.

CHAPTER 11

HOW TO TRAIN LEADERS

"And the things you have heard me say in the presence of many witnesses entrust to reliable men who will be qualified to teach others" (2 Tim. 2:2).

As you continue to minister in a man's life in helping him become a leader of a disciple-making team, you will need to concentrate on some specific training objectives (in the same way as you did earlier—Chapter 6 and Appendix 1, Chapter 9). They are not that much different from what you have been doing all along. They require no radical change of direction, for some of them are an extension of what you have done previously. They will not lead you down an altogether new path in a new direction with a new emphasis. They are the natural outgrowth and the next logical step in the training process.

Again, you should study these nine objectives and determine which ones your man needs. (And different men with whom you are working will need different ones.) Add to them or delete some; adapt as you feel is necessary. But remember that in one form or another these qualities should characterize a leader of a disciple-making team.

Developing Depth in His Life

The first objective is simply the continuation of something you began the day your man was converted to Christ. You continue to work on his spiritual depth, strength of character, and a fuller and richer knowledge of God. The key is understanding and knowing God. "Let not a wise man boast of his wisdom, and let not the mighty man boast of his might, let not a rich man boast of his riches; but let him who boasts boast of this, that he understands and knows Me, that I am the Lord who exercises lovingkindness, justice, and righteousness on earth; for I delight in these things" (Jer. 9:23-24).

The apostle Paul also had this as the heart cry of his own life:

> [For my determined purpose is] that I may know Him—that I may progressively become more deeply and intimately acquainted with Him, perceiving and recognizing and understanding [the wonders of His Person] more strongly and more clearly. And that I may in that same way come to know the power outflowing from His resurrection [which it exerts over believers]; and that I may so share His sufferings as to be continually transformed [in spirit into His likeness even] to His death (Phil. 3:10, *Amplified*).

If the man is to be used of God as a leader of a team of workers ("harvest workers"), his life must be lived in the secret place of intimate communion with Jesus Christ. His source of guidance, wisdom, strength to endure, and spiritual power to achieve comes from God alone. Let there be no mistake about this. He may attend management seminars by the scores; he may go to every leadership institute available; he may read dozens of books by various experts in the fields of organization, executive behavior, and use of time. But unless he continues to seek the Lord, his whole life and ministry will turn to ashes.

King Uzziah is a frightening and enlightening illustration of this. "And he continued to seek God in the days of Zechariah, who had understanding through the vision of God; and as long as he sought the Lord, God prospered him" (2 Chron. 26:5). He started well. He did well in the wars against Israel's enemies (2 Chron. 26:6-8). He became well known and it went to his head. "But when he became strong, his heart was so proud that he acted corruptly, and he was unfaithful to the Lord his God" (2 Chron. 26:16). To be a leader, a man must have developed in his daily walk with God.

Discovering His Vocation and Gifts
The second area where you must concentrate is helping your

potential leader discover and develop his gifts and settle in his own mind his personal calling from God. His calling will determine which road he takes in his service for Christ. Most of the men you train will remain laymen and serve the Lord in that capacity.

This is a high and noble calling from God. Contrary to the popular notion that to serve God effectively you must be a fulltime Christian worker, when the roll call of the mighty men of God down through the ages is called, the ones who stand up to be counted are almost all laymen (see Heb. 11). The prophet Samuel is listed among them, but the rest of God's heroes of the faith are men who served Him in the rough and tumble of everyday life.

His vocation. The unscriptural idea that a person must be a pastor, missionary, or "full-time" Christian worker if he is truly sold out to Christ has done untold damage to the cause of Jesus. Many men who would have been powerful and influential witnesses for Christ as laymen have been squeezed into the unnatural mold (for them) of the clerical robe and are frustrated and hindered for the rest of their lives.

Some of your men will feel the call of God on their lives to enter the full-time ministry. They will need counsel as to whether they should go to a theological school and if so which one. Should the man go to seminary or to a Bible institute or college? Determine these things prayerfully with him.

When a man leaves your side to enter his studies, don't abandon him. Pray for him. Visit him. Spend a generous amount of your time keeping him up to date on the progress of the disciple-making team and the results of the ministry in which he had participated.

The pattern generally is this: *Most* will continue as laymen; *some* will enter full-time service. Note how Paul said it, "It was he who gave *some* to be apostles, *some* to be prophets, *some* to be evangelists, and *some* to be pastors and teachers, to prepare God's people for works of service, so that the body of Christ may be built up" (Eph. 4:11-12). Let me reemphasize: those who are called to serve the Lord as laymen have every bit as high and noble calling as their brothers in the clergy. They are not second-class citizens.

His gifts. Your help and prayers are also needed to enable the potential leader to discover and develop his spiritual gift or gifts. Study and pray over the lists of gifts given in the Bible (see Rom. 12:6-8; 1 Cor. 12:4-11, 28-31; Eph. 4:11-12), and together try to help him to discover what his may be. He may have the gift of evangelism, the gift of teaching, the gift of administration, or one or more of the others. A simple guide that has been helpful to many is to ask these questions: when he carries out the ministry of a particular gift, (1) does he enjoy it? (2) are others helped? and (3) is the blessing of God evident? If the answer to all three questions is a resounding yes, it is probable that the man has this particular spiritual gift.

A common mistake is to try to guide him in the direction of some service that will make you look good and call attention to your ministry. What you must do is think of the man, *his* gifts, *his* abilities, *his* calling from God, and *his* ministry and effectiveness for Christ.

Building up His Strengths

You should spend the majority of your time building up his strengths, not correcting weaknesses, though weaknesses will need to be corrected. The best way to do that is to get the help of another trainer.

Two of the greatest aids in my own ministry to men have been cross evaluation and cross training. I value having a colaborer in the discipling ministry come alongside from time to time and spend some hours with the men I am training. I have a couple of weaknesses that are fairly common to many of us. I either look at a man through rose-colored glasses or through a microscope.

If I see the trainee through rose-colored glasses, I can see only his strong points. I need the help of another trainer of men to see things I can't. He can help me because he is not subjectively involved with the person I am training. Interestingly enough, my wife has been of great help to me in this area. Women can often see things we men can't, and I have learned to respect Virginia's observations. These helps from objective people will help me build up his strengths.

If my problem is that of looking at a man through a microscope, I need the help of another to get my perspective clear and help me see the man's good points and promising potential. The microscope has a way of magnifying flaws, and the evaluation of another can help clear the picture. We must remember that an expert builder carries on a positive ministry. To major on correcting errors is to get nowhere. We need to trust the grace of God to help us do this. Paul certainly did, and he wrote, "By the grace God has given me, I laid a foundation as an expert builder, and others are building on it. But each one should be careful how he builds" (1 Cor. 3:10).

Training Him in Leadership

Your potential leader must be trained to lead. He has served with you in the ministry and in so doing should now have a clear grasp of the vision of multiplication and should be proficient in his ministry skills. He has demonstrated a capacity and ability to commit the concepts of discipleship to faithful men who are able to repeat the process (see 2 Tim. 2:2). He should have further training in at least four areas.

Attitudes. The all-important and critical issue at this point is his attitude. He needs to be on guard against the swelling of his head, for that can be deadly. It is easy for him, even at this stage, to be filled with pride and so be tricked by the devil.

He also has to watch his attitude toward others. A new leader has the tendency to want to throw his weight around, to make sure others know who's in charge, to shout and demand, and in general do those things that are so obnoxious in the sight of God (and men). The reason for this type of behavior is a natural insecurity in the job and an attempt to cover that insecurity by bluster and a flurry of activity. And, of course, there is the desire to get on with the task at hand.

Consultations. The leader must learn to consult with his team, to bring the members into the planning stages of the ministry and decisionmaking. They will feel much more involved and look on their work as *their* ministry, which of course it is. But if the leader simply announces to the men what they are going to do without permitting them to be in on the thinking and discussions that led to that decision, he is being unwise. He may enlist their efforts, but he will lose their hearts. To bring team members into the discussion of plans and decisions will be a great advantage to the leader because of the involvement of many more good minds. They are then likely to arrive at much better plans as they contribute in concert together.

In the 1960s my wife and I were leading the Navigator ministry in the Midwest. We were living in Omaha and had developed a team of spiritually qualified workers. We would occasionally visit other states where discipleship ministries were under way. We had great fellowship on those trips and God used them in all our lives to teach us many lessons.

But then a problem developed. The car wore out and I began to look around for another one. I told the team I was looking for an automobile and asked them to pray for the right choice. Some of the members then suggested that we buy a nine-passenger station wagon. It would enable us to haul more people on the trips and our traveling Bible school would be enlarged.

I was against the idea. Station wagons rattled. You could not lock things securely out of sight because there was no trunk. They were heavier and burned more gas. They cost more. But we discussed it together. I saw their hearts were in it and began to see the wisdom of what they were saying. I finally told them I was wrong and they were right, and we would start looking for a station wagon.

We found one on which the team agreed, and the only thing left to do was raise the money. That didn't take long because their hearts were in it. It had been their idea, so it was their station wagon as much as it was mine. And we soon had money.

Buying the station wagon really helped the ministry. We devised a way in which we packed our clothes in paper sacks, put them under the seats, hauled ten people comfortably, and really put the thing to work. We drove over 60,000 miles the first year. Those men and women look back on those days as highly productive in their spiritual growth. Through that and other incidents, I learned the value of bringing the team in on planning and decisionmaking.

Practice. One of the best means of training a person in leadership is to let him put into practice, under limited supervision, that which he has been taught in previous training situations. This will help him gain confidence. It will also help him see for himself areas of strength and weakness. Then you can work out with him a simple plan that will build up his strengths and correct his weaknesses.

He will also be able to see himself in the role of a leader and how he relates to his peers and those whom he is leading. If he is given the opportunity to put it all to work, he will soon learn valuable lessons that he could learn no other way. He will learn how . . .

- to manage himself.
- to manage his time.
- to manage the ministry.
- to evaluate his men.
- to manage his finances.
- to use his home in the ministry with proper respect and regard for his family.
- to relate productively with others in the Christian ministry.

Suggestions. To help him most effectively, here are some basic things you can do to develop a climate where he will thrive and grow as a leader. These come from my own experience, most of which I had to learn the hard way.

1. Let him know you believe in him, love him, and thank God for him.

2. Let him know that he is free to discuss with you whatever is on his mind.

3. Let him know that you are always available to him.

4. Let him know that he is important to the ministry.

5. Tell him about your own successes and failures.

6. Set a high standard of performance for him. Otherwise your approval will mean nothing to him.

7. Keep yourself informed about his ministry. It is devastating when men say of their leader, "He doesn't know what is going on around here."

8. Keep some pressure on. Make sure he is involved in something that extends him a little beyond what he knows he can do. It is urgent that you really know your man. Too much too soon, and he can become frustrated and discouraged; too little too late, and he will be unchallenged and "rest on his oars."

9. If he needs help, counsel him. Let him know you are

there to help; it is not "sink or swim."

10. If he lacks confidence, set up a situation and ask him, "What would you do?" He will learn he can make decisions and he will soon be able to assume more responsibility.

11. Review his progress. Be generous and sincere in your praise; be loving and gentle in your correction.

Much of leadership training is a matter of involvement with those with whom you are working. Training is taxing work, but it is necessary.

Taking Steps That Stretch His Faith

Help the potential leader take steps that stretch his faith. Give him projects that cause him to depend on the Lord. I remember the first time I was responsible for the book table at a weekend conference. It appeared to me to be an awesome responsibility. I prayed; I sought counsel from others who had done it; I tried to accumulate a list of books that were old standbys; I studied catalogs of current books authored by men who had ministered to us in the past. The upshot of it was that God undertook and the book table ministry that weekend turned out well. But it really stretched my faith.

Jesus did that with His men. On the Sea of Galilee, when a great storm arose and waves beat into the little ship so that it filled with water, the faith of the apostles failed and they cried out, "Master, Master, we're going to drown!" (Luke 8:24). After Jesus had calmed them and the storm, He asked them why they were afraid and, "Where is your faith?" (Luke 8:25). The classroom was a boat; the curriculum was a storm; the lesson was on faith. Through it all they were helped and strengthened.

One of the best ways to stretch a man beyond his present ability and capacity is to put him to work. Jesus did that. "Calling the Twelve to him, he sent them out two by two and gave them authority over evil spirits" (Mark 6:7).

The men had been following Jesus and learning. It was not time to increase their capacity for further training and their ability for service. When you are involved with your men, you will observe that from time to time they seem to hit a learning plateau. That is the time to thrust them into something that really stretches them.

A long training experience of a week-long Bible conference can give you the feeling of being spiritually stuffed, but an opportunity to give your testimony or become involved in someone's life will soon bring back your hunger for the things of God. You can sharpen the spiritual appetites of your men by keeping them busy in the ministry of sharing their lives.

Refining His Ministry Skills

"The apostles gathered around Jesus and reported to him all they had done and taught" (Mark 6:3;). Wouldn't it have been exciting to have been at that debriefing session, heard the reports of those men, and listened to what Jesus told them?

Your men need the same opportunities for sharing and evaluating. They need to talk over with you the principles involved in starting and maintaining a discipleship ministry. They need to discuss the planning process and how to organize a team of men for the ministry. They need to go over the principles of leadership and learn how to evaluate the progress of the ministry and the effectiveness of the team.

Take all the time necessary to make sure you listen to your man when he comes to you and that he feels he has had your ear. Don't be afraid to ask questions and don't be startled by some of the questions he might ask you. If he asks a question that might sound a bit elementary, don't respond with the attitude, "You should know that. I taught you that six months ago!" Learning is a tedious process and sometimes lessons are missed or need to be gone over from another approach. Your job is to help the potential leader learn to do his ministry.

Learning Discernment

To learn to be a discerning person is critical for a young leader. When he begins his ministry on his own, there will be a multitude of demands on his time. Solomon said, "The naive believes everything, but the prudent man considers his steps" (Prov. 14:15). The leader will have to learn to sort out the productive from the fruitless, the best from the good, the truly important from that which merely has an urgent sound. The thing that will actually multiply the number of disciples is often disguised in a cloak of seeming irrelevance. The trained eye can see through the mask. And by way of contrast, someone will come along with a program that sounds terrific, but underneath it's a waste of time.

He will need discernment to sort out all this and know when to say yes and when to say no. By means of prayer, godly counsel, the Word of God, and a clear vision of the job to be done, the Holy Spirit will lead him step by step down the path of productive service. To earn the "well done" of Jesus will take discernment to avoid the tyranny of the urgent in favor of a solid ministry.

Moses, the man of God, prayed:

> As for the days of our life, they contain seventy years, or if due strength, eighty years, yet their pride is but labor and sorrow; for soon it is gone and we fly away. . . . So teach us to number our days, that we may present to Thee a heart of wisdom. . . . And let the favor of the Lord our God be upon us; and do confirm for us the work of our hands; yes, confirm the work of our hands (Ps. 90: 10, 12, 17).

Learning Communication Skills

The leader needs to learn to communicate truth simply and clearly. It is a common failing among men starting out in a speaking ministry to complicate things or to try to get across too much in too short a time. The objective is to see truth assimilated into the life, not to fill his head full of facts.

The Scriptures tell us that Jesus spoke with power. "They were amazed at his teaching, because his message had authority" (Luke 4:32). Some seem to believe that to speak with power means to speak loudly and forcibly, to pound the podium, or to stamp your feet. The reason we know the word of Jesus was with power was that when He spoke things happened. That's power—to see change for the better, to see new directions set, to see lives cleaned up, families reunited, old habits broken, to see commitments made that last, to see men and women gain a hunger for fellowship with Jesus Christ, and to see people beginning to dig into the Word of God and spend time on their knees in prayer.

Two Gospel statements give us insight into the reason for the power of the preaching of Jesus. "All spoke well of him and were amazed at the gracious words that came from his lips" (Luke 4:22). He spoke with a graciousness that won the hearts of His hearers. He spoke the truth openly and at times it was sharp and cutting. But there was a graciousness about His speech that was a wonder to behold.

The second statement was recorded by Mark. "The people were amazed at his teaching, because he taught them as one who had authority, not as the teachers of the law" (Mark 1:22). He spoke with authority. When a young leader speaks with the truth of the Word of God as his authority and speaks under the influence of the Holy Spirit, his message will have power.

Having a Good Doctrinal Foundation

If a man is to lead workers in a disciple-making ministry, he must have a good doctrinal foundation. Many good men get sidetracked by fuzzy or false doctrine. Some talk about the practical matters of Scripture on one hand and then the doctrinal issues on the other. This is not a good distinction. My experience in working with men has taught me that laying a good, solid, deep, doctrinal foundation in a man's life is one of the most practical as well as important things I can do. The devil is a subtle enemy, constantly on the alert to lead men astray. As you discuss the great truths of Scripture with the men you are training, you can discern what kind of grasp they have on those things and then go to work on what is lacking in them.

Here's a simple plan for a doctrinal study. Ask the person with whom you are working to type out on a card every passage he can find that related to the doctrine he is studying. Then ask him to lay these cards out on a table and meditate on them to see how certain passages relate to each other and what emphasis they bring to bear on the subject. After a week or so of meditation and relating these passages to one another, have him choose eight or ten of the ones that seem to be key and memorize them. This gives him his own personal study on the subject directly from the Scriptures and because he has memorized the key passages, he will have a good grasp of them for the rest of his life.

The apostle Paul spoke of the urgency of maturity and knowledge of the Scriptures. "Then we will no longer be infants, tossed back and forth by the waves, and blown here and there by every wind of teaching and by the cunning and craftiness of men in their deceitful scheming" (Eph. 4:14).

* * *

With these nine qualities built into his life, your potential leader of a disciple-making team should be ready to launch forth on his own. But your work is not finished. Your prayers and counsel are still needed, but you have trained him in the major areas of life for an effective ministry. You have done what you could to fulfill the responsibility of an expert builder.

CHAPTER 12

CONFIDENT AND UNASHAMED

"I tell you the truth, unless a kernel of wheat falls to the ground and dies, it remains only a single seed. But if it dies, it produces many seeds" (John 12:24).

When a person comes to Christ, he needs someone to feed him and help him learn how to feed himself from the Word of God. No one is alarmed over the fact that a brand new babe in Christ needs that kind of help. But the thing that should alarm us is that there are some people who need that sort of help year after year.

The writer to the Hebrews said:

> Though by this time you ought to be teachers, you need someone to teach you the elementary truths of God's Word all over again. You need milk, not solid food! Anyone who lives on milk, being still an infant, is not acquainted with the teaching about righteousness. But solid food is for the mature, who by constant use have trained themselves to distinguish good from evil (Heb. 5:12-14).

To help a person progress from these first faltering steps after his conversion to a place of leadership requires years of patient care, training, and prayer. And it is costly.

One of my favorite books is *Streams in the Desert,* and one of its devotional sections spoke of the cost of being a follower of Jesus Christ.

Shining is always costly. Light comes only at the cost of that which produces it. An unlit candle does no shining. Burning must come before shining. We cannot be of great use to others without cost to ourselves. Burning suggests suffering. We shrink from pain. . . . "The glory of tomorrow is rooted in the drudgery of today." Many want the glory without the cross, the shining without the burning, but crucifixion comes before coronation.[1]

Following these remarks was a poem that struck a responsive chord in my heart.

Have you heard the tale of the aloe plant,
    Away in the sunny clime?
By humble growth of a hundred years
    It reaches its blooming time;
And then a wondrous bud at its crown
    Breaks into a thousand flowers;
This floral queen, in its blooming seen,
    Is the pride of the tropical bowers,
But the plant to the flower is sacrifice,
    For it blooms but once, and it dies.

Have you further heard of the aloe plant,
    That grows in the sunny clime;
How every one of its thousand flowers,
    As they drop in the blooming time,
Is an infant plant that fastens its roots
    In the place where it falls on the ground,
And as fast as they drop from the dying stem,
    Grow lively and lovely around?
By dying, it liveth a thousand-fold
    In the young that spring from the death of the old.

Have you heard the tale of the pelican,
    The Arabs' Gimel el Bahr,
That lives in the African solitudes,
    Where the birds that live lonely are?
Have you heard how it loves its tender young,
    And cares and toils for their good,
It brings them water from mountain far,
    And fishes the seas for their food.
In famine it feeds them—what love can devise!
    The blood of its bosom—and, feeding them, dies.

Have you heard this tale—the best of them all—
    The tale of the Holy and True,

He dies, but His life, in untold souls
　　Lives on in the world anew;
His seed prevails, and is filling the earth,
　　As the stars fill the sky above.
He taught us to yield up the love of life,
　　For the sake of the life of love.
His death is our life, His loss is our gain;
　　The joy for the tear, the peace for the pain.[2]

Let's look at this matter of cost and training from the viewpoint
of the pastor who has the responsibility for the flock of God.
The apostle Paul stated:

> Do everything without complaining or arguing, so
> that you may become blameless and pure, children of
> God without fault in a crooked and depraved generation,
> in which you shine like stars in the universe as you hold
> out the word of life—in order that I may boast on the day
> of Christ that I did not run or labor for nothing (Phil.
> 2:14-16).

Here the apostle encouraged the Philippians to do things with
a cheery spirit and not spend their time in fruitless grumbling
and complaining. He told them to do this as they were holding
out the Word of life to others.

The reason he was so concerned about this was because of
his fear that he might "run or labor for nothing." Does that
mean that unless these people, for whom the apostle felt a
personal spiritual responsibility, learned how to share the
Word with others, he would feel that he had run and labored
for nothing? That is a sobering and challenging thought.

In the same vein, notice what John said, "And now, dear
children, continue in him, so that when he appears we may be
confident and unashamed before him at his coming" (1 John
2:28). Is the apostle saying that unless these people learn to
continue in Christ—that is, have an ongoing, daily relationship
with Him through the Word and prayer—that when John sees
Jesus at His coming he will be ashamed before Him? That is a
disturbing and challenging thought.

I shared these verses with a friend who pastors a church in
the suburb of a large city. He read and reread Philippians 2:16
and 1 John 2:28 and almost became ill. He looked at me and
said, "LeRoy, what am I doing? My people are not being

trained to share the Word with others or to live a deep abiding life in Christ."

He saw the truth taught in these passages in light of his current ministry and was tempted to walk off the job. But he also caught the vision of pouring his life into the lives of a few people and leading them into the steps of discipleship, workers, and leadership. Today he is not haunted by the thoughts expressed in those two passages.

In light of these things, take a good look at what John said earlier:

> I write to you, dear children,
> because your sins have been forgiven on
> account of his name.
> I write to you, fathers,
> because you have known him who is
> from the beginning.
> I write to you, young men,
> because you have overcome the evil one.
> I write to you, dear children,
> because you have known the Father.
> I write to you, fathers,
> because you have known him who is
> from the beginning.
> I write to you, young men,
> because you are strong,
> and the Word of God lives in you,
> and you have overcome the evil one.
> (1 John 2:12-14)

He started out by writing to the "children," people who knew very little other than that their sins were gone. He also wrote to them because they had come to know the Father. He then wrote to "fathers," those who had *really* come to know Him. Finally, he spoke to "young men" and reminded them that they were strong through the Word of God and had overcome the evil one. The children just knew the Father, the young men through the Word were able to overcome the evil one, and the fathers knew the Lord intimately.

One of the key things you can do to help your people is to guide them from being children to young manhood to being fathers. And the way they become overcomers is to get the Word of God into their hearts and lives.

This reminds us of what Paul said to the Thessalonians, "And we also thank God continually because, when you received the Word of God, which you heard from us, you accepted it not as the word of men, but as it actually is, the Word of God, which is at work in you who believe" (1 Thess. 2:13). Paul said that the Word of God was now set in operation in them like a huge dynamo, exercising its superhuman power. I shared this passage with a pastor once, and he told me, "LeRoy, it seems to me like you're some sort of a fanatic on getting people into the Word and getting the Word into their lives."

I told him that I was not a fanatic about getting the Word of God into the lives of people and letting it dwell there richly, but rather I was a *wild-eyed* fanatic in trying to get this done. I have seen what the Word of God has done in the hearts of hundreds of people through the years and the tremendous effect it has had on their lives.

The problem is that this cannot be accomplished wholesale. It cannot be done through a program. It is attained through individual, personal attention to people in helping them actually do these things and work these principles into their lives so it is part of them daily.

As soon as we start talking about giving people personal, individual attention, several problems arise. One is the problem of time. Most people today are already too busy. They are doing more than they have time for. What we must realize is that disciple making does not add to the time squeeze but helps resolve it. If the pastor ministers to a core of spiritually qualified men and women, *they* can begin carrying some of the burden and load. *They* can carry on some of the ministry.

Another problem is that of cliques. The pastor must consider how to avoid being criticized for seemingly showing favoritism. I once challenged a young pastor to find the most interested people in his congregation and begin helping them in their prayer lives and teaching them how to feed on the Word of God for themselves. But he was concerned about this matter of favoritism. So I suggested that he announce to the entire congregation on Sunday morning that he was starting a discipleship class at six o'clock Monday mornings for anyone who wanted to come. He already had two or three men in mind, so he went to them privately and encouraged them to attend. But in addition to those he extended an invitation to the entire congregation. Everyone knew that a discipleship class was starting and everyone had the opportunity to come.

Naturally, only those who were spiritually hungry showed up. Later, two or three dropped out, but those who stayed became real stalwarts in the church.

One of the best ways a pastor can get this ministry started is by giving priority to the men on his board of elders or deacons. The pastor who wants to disciple people successfully in his church must try to reach the existing leadership. The elders and/or deacons are just the ones with whom to start. If these men can be reached and trained, the pastor is well on his way to silencing criticism and other negative reactions within the congregation.

Another thing the pastor can do is use some creativity in determining how he can best utilize existing organizations and programs to aid in his disciple-making objectives. One of the ways to do this would be to use the church organizations (such as the Sunday school, men's organizations, and women's circles) and slowly redesign them to contribute to the disciple-making ministry. Actual discipling cannot be done on a large scale with these large groups, but we must realize that out of these groups able men and women will emerge.

A pastor who had been in such a ministry for three and a half years told me that in his congregation the most open and teachable people were a group of young men who were not members of any official board or responsible for any functions. Because of their openness and availability, he began with them. Now, three and a half years later, these men are beginning to assume positions of leadership in the church and are doing an excellent job of it.

His testimony teaches us that there is no hard and fast rule to follow. What we must do is to take each situation as it comes to us and go from there creatively. If board members are eager and responsive, then they should be trained for leadership. However, if they don't see the value of this, possibly the Lord has a few others in the congregation who would be responsive.

The pastor must stay on his knees and follow the example of Jesus (see Mark 3:14). So spend a night in prayer, asking the

Lord for the right men and women to involve in your ministry.
Despite the possible problems with this approach, we must
realize that discipling people is not an option or a suggestion,
but a command. It is the essential part of the Great Commission (see Matt. 28:19). We must seek the Lord on our knees and
let Him give us new and fresh ideas.

* * *

Some of the material in this book may not be relevant to your
situation at this time. Some of you may wish that I had gone
into greater detail on some matters and less on others. It's hard
to envision every possible situation. Possibly there are some
things that are not suited for your particular ministry.

Even though there may be some things in this book that
you cannot *adopt*, you may find ways to *adapt* some of them
into your life and ministry. Let this book serve as a reference to
methods that have worked around the world and are based on
the teachings of the Word of God. May the Holy Spirit use it to
raise up thousands of spiritually qualified workers for the glory
of Jesus Christ.

Notes

[1]Mrs. Charles E. Cowman, *Streams in the Desert* (Grand Rapids,
Mich.: Zondervan Publishing House), April 26, pp. 128-29.
[2]Ibid., 129-30.

APPENDIX 1

TRAINING OBJECTIVES
FOR A DISCIPLE

The training objectives for a disciple were listed in Chapter 6, their philosophy explained, and two of them described in detail. This appendix, which is an integral part of Chapter 6, spells out the details of each objective.

The format is to explain each objective briefly, to suggest some specific activities, to recommend pertinent materials, and to list applicable Scriptures. Space is left at the end of each section for you to add your own activities, materials, and Scriptures.

They are given in the same order as listed in Chapter 6, but the order is not necessarily sequential. Since each person is a unique individual and must be dealt with as such, you will want to adapt these to individual needs.

Topic 1 — ASSURANCE OF SALVATION

Training Objective:
> He will be able confidently to express to another person his own assurance of salvation based on his personal faith in Christ and one or more promises from the Word.

Activities:
1. Go over the gospel message with him again.
2. Ask him to tell you how he knows he is a Christian.
3. Observe how he explains his conversion experience to another person.
4. Do a Bible study with him on assurance of salvation.
5. _____
6. _____

Materials:
1. *Beginning with Christ* (NavPress), Section 1
2. *Lessons on Assurance* (NavPress), Chapter 1
3. *Studies in Christian Living* (NavPress), Book 1, Chapter 1
4. LeRoy Eims, *What Every Christian Should Know About Growing* (Victor Books), pages 51-53
5. Paul Hutchens, *The Know-so Christian* (Back to the Bible)
6. M. C. Griffiths, *Christian Assurance* (InterVarsity Press)
7. _____
8. _____

Scripture:
1. 1 John 5:13   We can know we're Christians
2. John 1:12,13   Based on the work of Christ
3. 1 John 5:11-12   The promise of the Word
4. Romans 8:16   The witness of the Spirit
5. _____ _____
6. _____ _____

Topic 2 — THE QUIET TIME

Training Objective:
He will have a daily quiet time, consisting of reading the Word and praying.

Activities:
1. Have a quiet time with him.
2. Share some blessings you have received from your own quiet time with him.
3. Tell him why you have it and show him how.
4. Pray through a psalm together.
5. Encourage him to share his quiet time with others.
6. _____
7. _____

Materials:
1. Robert D. Foster, *Seven Minutes with God* (NavPress)
2. *Devotional Diary* (NavPress)
3. *Studies in Christian Living* (NavPress), Book 2, Chapter 3
4. Mrs. Charles E. Cowman, *Streams in the Desert* (Zondervan)
5. Theodore Epp, *Beginning the Day with God* (Back to the Bible)
6. Theodore Epp, *Secrets of Christian Growth* (Back to the Bible)
7. *This Morning with God* (InterVarsity Press)
8. A. W. Tozer, *The Pursuit of God* (Christian Literature Crusade)
9. _____
10. _____

Scripture:
1. Mark 1:35   The example of Jesus
2. Genesis 19:27   The example of Abraham
3. Exodus 34:2,3   The example of Moses

4.	Psalm 5:3	The example of David
5.	Daniel 6:10	The example of Daniel
6.	1 Corinthians 1:9	Called to fellowship with Jesus
7.	_____	_____
8.	_____	_____

Topic 3 — VICTORY OVER SIN

Training Objective:

He knows how to experience victory over temptation through reliance on the Holy Spirit and trusting promises from the Word of God. This is evidenced by his clear testimony of a recent triumph over a specific temptation.

Activities:

1. Share a recent victory over sin with him.
2. Go over 1 Corinthians 10:13 with him in detail.
3. Memorize Psalm 119:9,11 with him.
4. _____
5. _____

Materials:

1. *Beginning with Christ* (NavPress), Section 3
2. *Lessons on Assurance* (NavPress) Chapter 3
3. Studies in Christian Living (NavPress), Book 2, Chapter 1, Questions 12-21
4. Theodore Epp, *Steps to Spiritual Victory* (Back to the Bible)
5. _____
6. _____

Scripture:

1.	1 Corinthians 10:13	A way of relief promised
2.	1 Corinthians 15:57	Victory through Jesus
3.	Isaiah 41:13	God's help promised
4.	_____	_____
5.	_____	_____

Topic 4 — SEPARATION FROM SIN

Training Objective:

He is taking steps to separate from sin by avoiding it, memorizing passages such as 2 Corinthians 6:17-18, praying about it, and soliciting the prayers of others.

Activities:

1. Pray with him about this activity.
2. Pray for him specifically.
3. Share a personal victory over besetting sin with him.
4. Get him into fellowship with victorious people.
5. Read and pray over 2 Corinthians 6:14-16 with him.

6. _____
7. _____

Materials:
1. *Beginning with Christ* (NavPress), Section 4
2. *Lessons on Assurance* (NavPress), Chapter 4
3. *Studies in Christian Living* (NavPress), Book 2, Chapter 1, Questions 22-25
4. John Stott, *Men Made New* (InterVarsity Press)
5. _____
6. _____

Scripture:
1. 1 John 1:5—2:2   Walking in the light
2. James 1:12   Persevering in trials
3. 2 Timothy 2:19-22   Departing from iniquity
4. Romans 6:12-14   Sin should not dominate us
5. 1 John 2:15-16   We should not love the world
6. Romans 12:2   Don't be conformed to the world
7. _____   _____
8. _____   _____

Topic 5—CHRISTIAN FELLOWSHIP

Training Objective:
He attends church, a Bible study group, and a prayer group.

Activities:
1. Find out his church background.
2. Take him to church with you.
3. Invite him to dinner to meet other Christians.
4. Involve him in a Bible study group.
5. Share with him why you go to church.
6. _____
7. _____

Materials:
1. *Studies in Christian Living* (NavPress), Book 3, Chapter 1
2. *Going on with Christ* (NavPress), Section 6
4. LeRoy Eims, *What Every Christian Should Know About Growing* (Victor Books), pages 57, 58, 158-160
5. A. W. Tozer, *Of God and Men* (Christian Publications)
6. _____
7. _____

Scripture:
1. Acts 2:42   Example of the early church
2. 1 John 1:3   Fellowship together
3. Hebrews 10:24-25   Not to forsake fellowship
4. Psalm 122:1   Go to church with gladness
5. _____   _____
6. _____   _____

Topic 6 — THE BIBLE

Training Objective:
    He is learning the books of the Bible and shares his belief in its inspiration openly.

Activities:
1. Help him obtain an accurate recent translation.
2. Show him how to use a concordance.
3. Show him how to use marginal notes, cross-references, and other helps in the Bible.
4. _____
5. _____

Materials:
1. *Going on with Christ* (NavPress), Section 2
2. *Lessons on Christian Living* (NavPress), Chapter 2
3. *Studies in Christian Living* (NavPress), Book 3, Chapter 2
4. LeRoy Eims, *What Every Christian Should Know About Growing* (Victor Books), Chapter 2
5. Walter A. Henrichsen, *Understand: A Straightforward Approach to Interpreting the Bible* (NavPress)
6. D. M. Lloyd-Jones, *Authority* (InterVarsity Press)
7. _____
8. _____

Scripture:
1. 2 Timothy 3:16-17   Inspiration of the Bible
2. 2 Peter 1:21   The Bible came by God's will
3. Matthew 22:29   Danger of not knowing the Scriptures
4. Psalm 19:7-11   Descriptions of God's Word
5. Psalm 119:160   The Word is true and eternal
6. Psalm 119:105   It is a lamp and a light
7. _____   _____
8. _____   _____

Topic 7 — HEARING THE WORD

Training Objective:
    He will hear the Word preached and taught, and will take notes on at least one message per week.

Activities:
1. Go to church together.
2. Teach him the value of notetaking.
3. Share with one another what you received out of the sermon.
4. _____
5. _____

Materials:
1. *Studies in Christian Living* (NavPress), Book 3, Chapter 3, Questions 13-15
2. _____
3. _____

Scripture:
1. Proverbs 28:9   Hearing a key to answered prayer
2. Jeremiah 22:29   The call to hear the Word
3. Luke 19:48   Hear attentively
4. _____   _____
5. _____   _____

Topic 8 — READING THE WORD

Training Objective:
He will systematically read his Bible.

Activities:
1. Share some personal blessings from your reading with him.
2. Read a section of the Bible together.
3. Get him started reading a New Testament book (Mark or John).
4. _____
5. _____

Materials:
1. *Studies in Christian Living* (NavPress), Book 3, Chapter 3, Questions 1-12, 16-19
3. *Bible Reading Plan* (NavPress)—notebook pages
3. LeRoy Eims, *What Every Christian Should Know About Growing* (Victor Books), page 31
4. _____
5. _____

Scripture:
1. 1 Timothy 4:13   Read carefully
2. Revelation 1:3   The blessings of reading
3. Deuteronomy 17:19   The need for daily reading
4. _____   _____
5. _____   _____

Topic 9 — BIBLE STUDY

Training Objective:
He will regularly complete his personal Bible study on time.

Activities
1. Share why you do Bible study with him.
2. Do an actual Bible study with him.
3. Show him the difference between study and reading.

    4. Get him started in personal Bible study.
    5. _____
    6. _____

Materials:
    1. *Studies in Christian Living* (NavPress), Book 3, Chapter 3, Questions 18, 19
    2. LeRoy Eims, *What Every Christian Should Know About Growing* (Victor Books), page 30
    3. _____
    4. _____

Scripture:
    1. Acts 17:11   Commendation for Bible study
    2. Proverbs 2:1-5   Study is like searching for treasure
    3. Ezra 7:10   The example of Ezra
    4. _____   _____
    5. _____   _____

Topic 10 — SCRIPTURE MEMORY

Training Objectives:
    He is regularly memorizing Scripture and maintaining adequate review.

Activities:
    1. Explain the personal blessings of Scripture memory.
    2. Memorize a verse together.
    3. Review your verses together.
    4. Check on his review plan.
    5. Have him meet others who are memorizing Scripture.
    6. _____
    7. _____

Materials:
    1. *Studies in Christian Living* (NavPress), Book 3, Chapter 3, Questions 20-23
    2. *Beginning with Christ* (NavPress)
    3. *Going on with Christ* (NavPress)
    4. *The Topical Memory System* (NavPress)
    5. LeRoy Eims, *What Every Christian Should Know About Growing* (Victor Books), page 26
    6. Dawson Trotman, *Coming to Christ Through Scripture Memory* (NavPress)
    7. _____
    8. _____

Scripture:
    1. Colossians 3:16   Memory enriches us
    2. Deuteronomy 6:6-7   Moses urges Scripture memory
    3. Matthew 4:4   The example of Christ

4. Psalm 37:31   It gives stability
5. Proverbs 7:1-3   Should be written on the heart
6. _____   _____
7. _____   _____

Topic 11 — MEDITATION ON THE WORD

Training Objective:
   He will be able to explain the meaning of meditation and a personal
   blessing from meditating on a recent memory verse.

Activities:
   1. Share a blessing from your own meditation with him.
   2. Go through a passage, visualize the context, and check with him
      regarding what the passage teaches (who, what, where, when, why,
      and how questions).
   3. Share with him a meditation plan.
   4. _____
   5. _____

Materials:
   1. *A Primer on Meditation* (NavPress)
   2. *Studies in Christian Living* (NavPress), Book 3, Chapter 3, Questions
      24-27
   3. LeRoy Eims, *What Every Christian Should Know About Growing* (Vic-
      tor Books), p. 32
   4. LeRoy Eims, *Winning Ways* (Victor Books), pages 123-24
   5. LeRoy Eims, *Be the Leader You Were Meant to Be* (Victor Books), page
      19
   6. Jim Downing, *Meditation: The Bible Tells You How* (NavPress)
   7. _____
   8. _____

Scripture:
   1. Psalm 1   Results of meditation
   2. Joshua 1:8   Promises to the one meditating
   3. Jeremiah 15:16   Meditation brings joy
   4. Philippians 4:8   Mental discipline of meditation
   5. _____   _____
   6. _____   _____

Topic 12 — APPLICATION OF THE WORD

Training Objective:
   He demonstrates a desire to apply the Word of God by writing and
   completing one or more specific applications.

Activities:
   1. Share an application you have written with him.
   2. Have him share a written application with you.

3. Pray over his and your applications.
4. _____
5. _____

Materials:
1. LeRoy Eims, *What Every Christian Should Know About Growing* (Victor Books), pages 56-57
2. Theodore Epp, *Christian Maturity – How?* (Back to the Bible)
3. _____
4. _____

Scripture:
1. James 1:22-25   We must do what the Word says
2. Psalm 119:56,60   Meditation leads to application
3. 2 Timothy 3:16-17   God's Word is profitable for life
4. Luke 6:46-49   Obedience is a sure foundation
5. _____   _____
6. _____   _____

Topic 13 — PRAYER

Training Objective:
He demonstrates a consistent prayer life by praying daily for a minimum of ten minutes and confidently participates in group prayer.

Activities:
1. Ask him to share some answers to prayer.
2. Observe what he prays for in a group situation.
3. Share Scriptures with him he can use in praying.
4. Pray with him, planned and spontaneous.
5. Help him develop a prayer list.
6. Ask him to pray for one of your needs.
7. Pray regularly with him at set times and "on the run."
8. Share your answers to prayer with him.
9. Take him to prayer groups.
10. Expose him to people of prayer.
12. _____
13. _____

Materials:
1. *Studies in Christian Living* (NavPress), Book 6, Chapter 3
2. Jerry Bridges, *How to Get Results through Prayer* (NavPress)
3. *Beginning with Christ* (NavPress), Section 2
4. *Lessons on Assurance* (NavPress), Chapter 2
5. E. M. Bounds, *Power through Prayer* (Moody)
6. Rosalind Rinker, *Conversational Prayer* (Zondervan)
7. LeRoy Eims, *What Every Christian Should Know About Growing* (Victor Books), Chapter 3
8. LeRoy Eims, *Winning Ways* (Victor Books), pages 134-35
9. LeRoy Eims, *Be the Leader You Were Meant to Be* (Victor Books), pages 21-23

10. J. Oswald Sanders, *Effective Prayer* (Moody)
11. _____
12. _____

Scripture:

1.	1 Thessalonians 5:17	Pray without ceasing
2.	Matthew 6:6	Pray privately
3.	John 17	The example of Christ
4.	James 5:17	Prayer brings results
5.	Philippians 4:6-7	Pray for personal concerns
6.	Matthew 21:22	Pray in faith
7.	1 John 3:22	Obedience is the condition for answered prayer
8.	Matthew 7:7	Keep asking, seeking, knocking
9.	Ephesians 6:18	Pray at all times for the saints
10.	_____	_____
11.	_____	_____

Topic 14 — PERSONAL TESTIMONY

Training Objective:

He has prepared a three-minute written testimony, including at least one Scripture, and has shared it with at least two non-Christians within one month.

Activities:

1. Share your testimony with him.
2. Have him share his testimony with you.
3. Study Acts 26 together; point out Paul's approach, personal background, and his meeting Jesus.
4. Take him witnessing with you.
5. While witnessing, draw out his testimony with questions.
6. Ask him to share his testimony with Christians (such as in a Bible study group).
7. Review his testimony as to content and clarity with him.
8. Pray with him about relatives and friends with whom he can share his testimony.
9. Pray that God would build this desire into his life.
10. Expose him to other Christians' testimonies.
11. _____
12. _____

Materials:

1. *Studies in Christian Living* (NavPress), Book 2, Chapter 4, Questions 12-21
2. Dawson Trotman, *Born to Reproduce* (NavPress)
3. Dawson Trotman, *Coming to Christ through Scripture Memory* (NavPress)
4. LeRoy Eims, *What Every Christian Should Know About Growing* (Victor Books), pages 104-106

5. _____
6. _____

Scripture:
1. Luke 8:38-39   Illustrating a changed life
2. Acts 26:1-23   Paul's testimony
3. John 9:25   The former blind man's testimony
4. 1 John 1:3   Declare what you've experienced
5. _____   _____
6. _____   _____

Topic 15 — LORDSHIP OF CHRIST

Training Objective:
He evidences a lordship commitment by having allowed Christ to control at least one uncommitted area of his life.

Activities:
1. *Ask him to read My Heart, Christ's Home* by Robert Munger.
2. Check his follow-through on application from his Bible study.
3. Share a personal testimony with him on how you made Christ your Lord.
4. Study Colossians 1:18 and Hebrews 1 with him.
5. Listen to the tape *The Worthiness of Christ* by George Sanchez (NavPress)
6. Counsel with him on the check chart on lordship, *Studies in Christian Living,* Book 2, page 14.
7. _____
8. _____

Materials:
1. Robert Munger, *My Heart, Christ's Home* (InterVarsity Press)
2. *Studies in Christian Living* (NavPress), Book 2, Chapter 2
3. LeRoy Eims, *What Every Christian Should Know About Growing* (Victor Books), Chapter 5
4. _____
5. _____

Scripture:
1. Luke 6:46   Obedience to Christ a necessity
2. Romans 12:1,2   Decisive commitment needed
3. Colossians 1:18   Christ must be preeminent
4. Hebrews 1:2   Christ is heir of all things
5. _____   _____
6. _____   _____

Topic 16 — FAITH

Training Objective:
He evidences the fruit of trusting God for specific needs.

Activities:
1. Share a fresh personal testimony with him on what God has done for you in response to faith.
2. Read through Hebrews 11 together.
3. _____
4. _____

Materials:
1. *Going on with Christ* (NavPress), Section 4
2. *Lessons on Christian Living* (NavPress) Chapter 4
3. LeRoy Eims, *What Every Christian Should Know About Growing* (Victor Books), pages 160-162
4. Russ Johnston, *God Can Make It Happen* (Victor Books)

Scripture:
1. Hebrews 11:6   Impossible to Please God without faith
2. Ephesians 6:16   Faith gives victory over Satan
3. 1 John 5:4   Faith overcomes the world
4. Romans 4:20-21   Faith glorifies God
5. _____   _____
6. _____   _____

Topic 17 — LOVE

Training Objective:
He shows love for others by having concern for them, acting in a loving manner, and doing something for a needy person (at least one during the week).

Activities:
1. Share with him a personal example.
2. Demonstrate love to him.
3. Share scriptural examples and principles with him.
4. Visit a hospital, rest home, and/or prison.
5. Do a study together on 1 Corinthians 13.
6. _____
7. _____

Materials:
1. *Studies in Christian Living* (NavPress), Book 4, Chapter 1
2. Henry Drummond, *The Greatest Thing in the World* (Revell)
3. LeRoy Eims, *What Every Christian Should Know About Growing* (Victor Books), pages 76-77
4. *Going on with Christ* (NavPress), Section 5
6. Francis Schaeffer, *The Mark of the Christian* (InterVarsity Press)
7. _____
8. _____

Scripture:
1. John 13:34-35   The command to love

2. 1 John 3:17-18   Love meets others' needs
3. John 15:13   Love means total sacrifice
4. 1 Corinthians 13:4-7 How to love others
5. 1 John 4:7-21   We are to love one another
6. _____ _____
7. _____ _____

Topic 18 — THE TONGUE

Training Objective:
He demonstrates control over his tongue.

Activities:
1. Share with him how you have controlled your tongue.
2. Do a Bible study on James 3 together.
3. _____
4. _____

Materials:
1. *Studies in Christian Living* (NavPress), Book 4, Chapter 3, Questions 1-8
2. LeRoy Eims, *What Every Christian Should Know About Growing* (Victor Books), pages 120-122
3. _____
4. _____

Scripture:
1. Ephesians 4:29   Speak only edifying words
2. Proverbs 26:20   Don't be a talebearer
3. Proverbs 18:6-7   A fool's mouth is his ruin
4. Psalm 71:15   The mouth is to praise God
5. Colossians 4:6   Speak gracious words
6. James 1:26   Control negative speech
7. James 3:1-12   Danger of an uncontrolled tongue
8. _____ _____
9. _____ _____

Topic 19 — THE USE OF TIME

Training Objective:
He demonstrates growth in the effective use of his time by forming and following a schedule.

Activities:
1. Work out a schedule with him.
2. Help him make the time effective through instruction.
3. Encourage him by praying with him for this area.
4. _____
5. _____

Materials:
1. *Tyranny of the Urgent* (InterVarsity Press)
2. *Studies in Christian Living* (NavPress), Book 4, Chapter 4, Questions 1-8
3. Jerry and Mary White, *Your Job—Survival or Satisfaction?* (Zondervan)
4. _____
5. _____

Scripture:
1. Ephesians 5:15-17   Redeeming the time
2. Psalm 90:10,12   Planning your time
3. Ecclesiastes 3:1   Priority of time
4. James 4:14   Brevity of life
5. Romans 13:11   Urgency of time
6. Proverbs 31:27   Not wasting time
7. _____ _____
8. _____ _____

Topic 20 — THE WILL OF GOD

Training Objective:
He shares how he made one major decision, utilizing biblical principles on knowing the will of God.

Activities:
1. Share a personal experience of finding God's will.
2. Have other Christians do the same.
3. Have him share with you how he makes major decisions.
4. _____
5. _____

Materials:
1. *Studies in Christian Living* (NavPress), Book 4, Chapter 4, Questions 17-28
2. Paul Little, *Finding God's Will* (InterVarsity Press)
3. LeRoy Eims, *What Every Christian Should Know About Growing* (Victor Books), pages 54-56
4. *Beginning with Christ* (NavPress), Section 5
5. *Lessons on Assurance* (NavPress), Chapter 5
6. G. C. Weiss, *How to Know the Will of God* (Back to the Bible)
7. Russ Johnston, *How to Know the Will of God* (NavPress)
8. _____
9. _____

Scripture:
1. Psalm 119:105   Direction through God's Word
2. Proverbs 15:22   Obtaining godly counsel
3. John 16:13   The Holy Spirit's ministry in our lives
4. Romans 12:1-2   God's will is good, pleasing, perfect

5. _____   _____
6. _____   _____

Topic 21 — Obedience

Training Objective:
He is learning to be an obedient Christian as evidenced by his carrying out specific Bible study applications.

Activities:
1. Discuss with him how to make specific applications.
2. Check up on his previous applications.
3. Share illustrations from your own life.
4. Share the results of one of your own Bible study applications.
5. _____
6. _____

Materials:
1. LeRoy Eims, *What Every Christian Should Know About Growing* (Victor Books), pages 70-71
2. Robert Munger, *My Heart, Christ's Home* (InterVarsity Press)
3. John Stott, *Being a Christian* (InterVarsity Press)

Scripture:
1. John 14:21   Love is proved by obedience
2. Job 17:9   Strength results from continued obedience
3. John 15:10,14   Obedience brings fruitfulness and pleases God
4. 1 Samuel 15:22   Obedience is better than sacrifice
5. Psalm 119:59-60   God wants instant obedience
6. James 4:17   Disobedience is sin
7. John 14:23   Incentive for obedience
8. _____   _____
9. _____   _____

Topic 22 — THE HOLY SPIRIT

Training Objective:
He is able to express through Scripture who the Holy Spirit is and how He helps us in our daily walk. He can explain to another person how to walk in the Spirit.

Activities:
1. Teach him who the Holy Spirit is by explaining the concept of the Trinity.
2. Pray with him, asking the Holy Spirit's guidance.
3. Observe and point out his areas of personal victory.
4. Set an example of praying for the Holy Spirit's control.
5. List items that grieve the Holy Spirit and quench Him.

6. _____
7. _____

Materials:
1. *Studies in Christian Living* (NavPress), Book 5, Chapter 2
2. LeRoy Eims, *What Every Christian Should Know About Growing* (Victor Books), pages 149-151
3. *Going on with Christ* (NavPress), Section 3
4. *Lessons on Christian Living* (NavPress), Chapter 3
5. John Stott, *Baptism and Fullness of the Holy Spirit* (InterVarsity Press)
6. _____
7. _____

Scripture:
1. John 14:16,17   He is the Comforter
2. Romans 8:26   He helps us pray
3. John 16:7,8   The ministry of the Spirit
4. Galatians 5:22-23   The fruits of the Spirit
5. Ephesians 5:18   Be filled with the Spirit
6. Romans 8:5-6   Spirit and flesh conflict
7. Romans 12:3-8   Gifts of the Holy Spirit
8. 1 Corinthians 12:13-14 Ministry of the Spirit
9. Zechariah 4:6   The power of the Spirit
10. Romans 8:16-17   Spirit bears us witness
11. John 16:13-15   Spirit glorifies Christ
12. John 15:26-27   The witness of the Spirit
13. _____   _____
14. _____   _____

Topic 23 — SATAN—KNOW YOUR ENEMY

Training Objective:
He expresses instances of personal victory over Satan by use of prayer and Scripture. He has shared how he has overcome an attack of Satan in his life by using the Word. He prays against Satan as a personal spiritual enemy.

Activities:
1. Ask about his biggest temptation.
2. Share some of your personal battles and victories.
3. Pray with him against Satan's attacks.
4. Review Bible passages on how Satan attacks.
5. Share your testimony on how you have overcome Satan's attack by using the Word.
6. Do a study together on Matthew 4:1-11.
7. Don't get him too fascinated with the subject.
8. _____
9. _____

Materials:
1. *Studies in Christian Living* (NavPress), Book 5, Chapter 3

2. LeRoy Eims, *What Every Christian Should Know About Growing* (Victor Books), pages 163-168
3. Theodore Epp, *How to Resist Satan* (Back to the Bible)
4. J. D. Pentecost, *Your Adversary the Devil* (Zondervan)
5. _____
6. _____

Scripture:

1.	Ephesians 6:10-18	Spiritual weapons for warfare
2.	2 Corinthians 10:3-5	Ours are not fleshly weapons
3.	1 John 4:4	Satan's power is limited
4.	1 Peter 5:8-9	Satan's action as the enemy
5.	John 8:44	Satan is a liar
6.	Isaiah 14:12-15	The fall of Satan
7.	1 John 3:8	Satan's works destroyed
8.	2 Corinthians 4:3-4	Satan's wiles
9.	2 Corinthians 2:11	We can know the enemy
10.	Matthew 4:4	Use of the Word to overcome the enemy
11.	_____	_____
12.	_____	_____

Topic 24 — DEALING WITH SIN

Training Objective:

He has identified a major area of sin in his life, having shared a plan for obtaining victory and is progressing positively.

Activities.

1. Share with him a means of victory.
2. Share some of your own problems and victories.
3. Pray with him about major areas of sin.
4. Share with him the danger of continuing in sin.
5. _____
6. _____

Materials:

1. LeRoy Eims, *What Every Christian Should Know About Growing* (Victor Books), Chapter 10
2. Robert Munger, *My Heart, Christ's Home* (InterVarsity Press)
3. _____
4. _____

Scripture:

1.	Colossians 3:9-10	Live a new life
2.	1 Peter 1:14-16	Holy behavior a must
3.	Ephesians 6:10-20	The whole armor of God
4.	Romans 13:14	Trusting Christ
5.	Mark 14:38	Watch and pray
6.	1 John 1:9	Confession

7. _____ _____
8. _____ _____

Topic 25 — ASSURANCE OF FORGIVENESS

Training Objectives:
  He will be able confidently to express to another person his own assurance
  of forgiveness based on one or more promises from the Word.

Activities:
  1. Ask him if he has experienced God's forgiveness for a sin.
  2. Have him make restitution in a personal conflict with another person.
  3. Share your own testimony of sin forgiven.
  4. _____
  5. _____

Materials:
  1. *Studies in Christian Living* (NavPress), Book 5, Chapter 4, Questions
     21-27
  2. *Beginning with Christ* (NavPress), Section 4
  3. *Lessons on Assurance* (NavPress), Chapter 4
  4. Tape *How to Experience God's Love and Forgiveness* by Bill Bright
     (Campus Crusade)
  5. _____
  6. _____

Scripture:
  1. 1 John 1;9   Forgiveness through confession
  2. Psalm 32:1   Blessing of forgiveness
  3. Matthew 5:23-24   Necessity of restitution
  4. Matthew 18:15   Necessity of restitution
  5. _____   _____
  6. _____   _____

Topic 26 — SECOND COMING OF CHIRST

Training Objective:
  He has expressed a new awareness of Christ's return and can share
  Scripture passages relating to it.

Activities:
  1. Ask him what he would do differently if Christ were to come today.
  2. Share how the second coming of Christ motivates you.
  3. _____
  4. _____

Materials:
  1. *Studies in Christian Living* (NavPress), Book 5, Chapter 5
  2. LeRoy Eims, *What Every Christian Should Know About Growing*
     (Victor Books, pages 151-154

3. Ord L. Morrow, *Behold He Cometh* (Back to the Bible)
4. Theodore Epp, *Why Must Jesus Come Again* (Back to the Bible)
5. G. T. Manley, *The Return of Jesus Christ* (InterVarsity Press)
6. Charles Ryrie, *The Living End* (Revell)
7. _____
8. _____

Scripture:
1. 1 Thessalonians 4:16-17 Christ's promise to return
2. John 14:2-3   He will receive us
3. 1 John 3:2-3   Challenge to our lives
4. Titus 2:11-14   Live godly lives
5. Revelation 19:11-16   His coming in glory
6. _____   _____
7. _____   _____

Topic 27 — WITNESSING

Training Objective:
He takes initiative to share the gospel clearly, using the Word.

Activities:
1. Read Dawson Trotman's testimony in *Born to Reproduce* and *Coming to Christ through Scripture Memory.*
2. Pray for conviction in witnessing.
3. Have him witness with another person.
4. Pray together for contacts.
5. Make and use a prayer list of non-Christian friends.
6. Allow him to observe you as you make contacts and witness.
7. Lead an evangelistic Bible study group.
8. Go witnessing together.
9. _____
10. _____

Materials:
1. *Studies in Christian Living* (NavPress), Book 6, Chapter 1
2. *The Bridge to Life* (NavPress)—a tract
3. Lorne Sanny, *The Art of Personal Witnessing* (Moody)
4. *The Four Spiritual Laws* (Campus Crusade)—a tract
5. Paul Little, *How to Give Away Your Faith* (InterVarsity Press)
6. John Stott, *Evangelism: Why and How* (InterVarsity Press)
7. LeRoy Eims, *Winning Ways* (Victor Books)
8. Robert E. Coleman, *The Master Plan of Evangelism* (Revell)
9. LeRoy Eims, *What Every Christian Should Know About Growing* (Victor Books), Chapter 1
10. _____
11. _____

Scripture:
1. Colossians 1:28-29   Proclaim Christ naturally
2. Romans 1:16   Not ashamed of the gospel

 3. 2 Timothy 4:1-2   Proclaim Christ at all times
 4. Proverbs 11:30   The wise win souls
 5. Acts 8:35   Use the Bible to present the gospel
 6. Proverbs 28:1   Boldness is necessary
 7. 1 Corinthians 15:3-4 The gospel described
 8. John 4   The example of Jesus and the woman
                        of Samaria
 9. Luke 19:10   Seek after sinners
10. _____   _____
11. _____   _____

Topic 28 — FOLLOW-UP

Training Objective:
   He has started praying that God would give him a person to follow up.

Activities:
   1. Share your own follow-up plan with him.
   2. Have him go with you when you follow up someone.
   3. Have him present *Beginning with Christ* to you.
   4. Pray with him over those with whom he is working.
   5. Pray together on the follow-up of a new convert.
   6. _____
   7. _____

Materials:
   1. *Studies in Christian Living* (NavPress), Book 6, Chapter 2
   2. Dawson Trotman, *Follow-up* (NavPress)
   3. Dawson Trotman, *Born to Reproduce* (NavPress)
   4. LeRoy Eims, *Winning Ways* (Victor Books), Chapter 12
   5. Michael Griffiths, *Encouraging New Christians* (InterVarsity Press)
   6. Gary W. Kuhne, *The Dynamics of Personal Follow-up* (Zondervan)
   7. _____
   8. _____

Scripture:
   1. Colossians 1:28   Present every man perfect in Christ
   2. 3 John 4   The joy of seeing people walking
                          with God
   3. 3 Timothy 2:2   Teaching a faithful man to reproduce
   4. 2 Timothy 1:3   Prayer in follow-up
   5. _____   _____
   6. _____   _____

Topic 29 — GIVING

Training Objective:
   He is giving regularly to the Lord's work.

Activities:
   1. Help him list scriptural principles on giving from Bible study.

2. Check with him as to how his plan of giving is working.
3. Work with him on an overall budget (if necessary).
4. Help him establish a plan for giving.
5. _____
6. _____

Materials:
1. *Studies in Christian Living* (NavPress), Book 6, Chapter 4
2. *Going on with Christ* (NavPress), Section 8
3. *Lessons on Christian Living* (NavPress), Chapter 8
4. LeRoy Eims, *What Every Christian Should Know About Growing* (Victor Books), pages 84-86
5. _____
6. _____

Scripture:
1. Proverbs 3:9-10   Give to God first
2. 2 Corinthians 9:6-8   Give joyfully
3. Luke 6:38   The blessings of giving
4. Proverbs 3:27   Give when you can
5. Galatians 6:6   Share resources with spiritual teachers
6. Malachi 3:10   Give and receive God's blessing
7. Proverbs 11:24-25   The generous man is blessed
8. 2 Corinthians 8:9   Though He was rich, Christ became poor for us
9. _____   _____
10. _____   _____

Topic 30 — WORLD VISION

Training Objectives:
He demonstrates an interest and concern in world vision through weekly prayer for missionaries and people of foreign countries. He gives to the monthly support of an overseas missionary.

Activities:
1. Introduce him to visiting foreign missionaries.
2. Pray with him, using missionary prayer letters.
3. Use a world map and pray for countries around the world.
4. Correspond with missionaries and learn of various mission fields and agencies with him.
5. Read and discuss missionary biographies and books on missions.
6. Share your missionary giving program with him.
7. _____
8. _____

Materials:
1. World map or globe or atlas
2. *Studies in Christian Living* (NavPress), Book 6, Chapter 5
3. Missionary prayer letters

4. Missionary biographies
5. Dawson Trotman, *Born to Reproduce* (NavPress)
6. Michael Griffiths, *You and God's Work Overseas* (InterVarsity Press)
7. _____
8. _____

Scripture:
   1. Matthew 9:35-38   Prayer for laborers in the fields of
                           the world
   2. Matthew 28:19-20   Make disciples everywhere
   3. Acts 1:8   Go to the ends of the earth
   4. Mark 16:15   Preach the gospel to all
   5. Luke 24:47   Go to all nations
   6. John 20:21   Jesus' commission to us, based on His
                           successful mission
   7. Isaiah 6:8   Willingness to go
   8. _____
   9. _____

APPENDIX 2

HOW TO MULTIPLY THE MINISTRY

This chart portrays the processes of helping a man (or a woman) go from being a convert or an untaught Christian to becoming a disciple, a worker, and a leader.

The first process is *evangelizing,* in which we witness to Jesus Christ and His work in our lives in obedience to His command: "*Go* into all the world *and preach* the good news to all creation" (Mark 16:15). The result of this process is a *convert* as God blesses our ministry of sharing the gospel.

The next process is *establishing.* "As you therefore have received Christ Jesus the Lord, so walk in Him, having been firmly rooted and now being built up in His and *established* in your faith, just as you were instructed, and overflowing with gratitude" (Col. 2:6,7, NASB). In this step we follow up the new convert, building into his life the characteristics of a disciple's life contained in your training objectives. The end result is a disciple who is now able to evangelize.

The next process is *equipping,* "And He gave some as apostles, and some as prophets, and some as evangelists, and some as pastors and teachers, for the *equipping* of the saints for the *work* of service, to the building up of the body of Christ" (Eph. 4:11,12, NASB). Here you work man-to-man with the disciple, leading him through your training objectives. The result of this process is a *worker*—a "harvest worker"—who is now able both to evangelize and establish, equipping other workers, which Jesus said are few and remain few to this day.

181

The final process is *in-depth personal training* after the pattern of Jesus. "He appointed twelve—designating them apostles—that *they might be with him* and that he might *send them out to preach*" (Mark 3:14). In this training you utilize the "with him" principle of spending concerted and quality time with the worker, taking him through your training objectives. The final result is a *leader* who is able to reproduce the whole process. He is able to evangelize the lost, establish the converts, equip the disciples, and spend in-depth training time with the workers, producing leaders of disciple-making teams.

Ultimately, a leader—a servant leader—is a man who can go to another pool of manpower and under the guidance of the Holy Spirit of God reproduce the kind of ministry in which he himself was raised up.

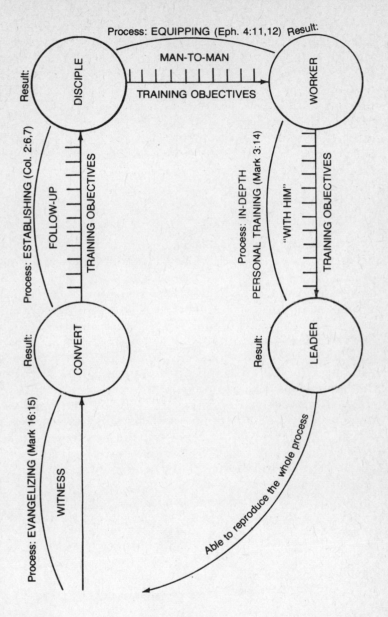

APPENDIX 3

PROFILES OF A CONVERT, DISCIPLE, WORKER, AND LEADER

This appendix provides profiles of each step of the disciple-making process. It can serve as a check on how you are progressing in each step. When you have led a person to Christ and want to see if his conversion was genuine, check him against the profile of a convert. As you begin working with the man in follow-up and building your training objectives into his life, check to see how you are doing by noting how he compares against the profile of a disciple. When he matches that profile, you have a disciple on your hands and are ready to see if he has the hunger and desire to proceed with the next process.

As you work man-to-man with a disciple and build your training objectives into his life, start checking to see how close and how fast he is coming to meeting the profile of a worker. When he does, you have a worker that might be ready to take the last step. As you work with him in building your leadership training objectives in his life, note how close he is to meeting the profile of a leader. When that occurs, you have a leader who is prepared to go out on his own and reproduce the whole process.

Profile of a Convert

1. He gives evidences of possessing new life (see 2 Cor. 5:17).
2. His attitude toward Jesus Christ is now favorable.
3. His attitude toward sin is now unfavorable.

Profile of a Growing Disciple

1. As a follower of Jesus Christ, he puts Christ first in the major areas of his life and is taking steps to separate from sin (see Luke 9:23; Rom. 12:1,2).

2. He continues in the Word through such means of intake as Bible study and Scripture memory; he is regular in applying the Word to his life with the help of the Holy Spirit (see John 8:31; James 1:22-25; Ps. 119:59).

3. He maintains a consistent devotional life and is growing in faith and intercessory prayer (see Mark 1:35; Heb. 11:6; Col. 4:2-4).

4. He attends church regularly and demonstrates Christ's love by identifying with and serving other believers (see Ps. 122:1; Heb. 10:25; John 13:34-35; 1 John 4:20-21; Gal. 5:13).

5. He is openly identified with Jesus Christ where he lives and works, manifests a heart for witnessing, gives his testimony clearly, and presents the gospel regularly with increasing effectiveness (see Matt. 5:16; Col. 4:6; 1 Peter 3:15).

6. He is a learner who is open and teachable (see Acts 17:11).

7. He is a visible follower and learner of Jesus Christ, and demonstrates consistency and faithfulness in all of the above areas (see Luke 16:10).

Profile of a Worker

1. He evidences growth in the virtues and skills outlined under *Profile of a Growing Disciple* (see 1 Peter 3:18).

2. He shows a growing compassion for the lost and demonstrates his ability to lead men to Christ personally (see Matt. 9:36-38; Rom. 1:6).

3. He is being used of God to establish believers who have become disciples, either personally or in a discipling group context (see Col. 1:28,29).

4. He is currently engaged in the task of making disciples (see Matt. 28:19).

5. Regular intake of the Word by all means and the quiet time are now habits in his life (see Phil. 4:9).

Profile of a Leader

1. He is an equipped worker who evidences growth in the virtues and skills listed under *Profile of a Worker*.

2. He has been used of God to help disciples become workers (see 2 Tim. 2:2).

3. He is banding and leading workers in evangelizing the lost and establishing believers (see Mark 1:38).

4. He displays faithfulness and integrity in his life and ministry (see 2 Tim. 2:19-21).

APPENDIX 4

THE TIME ELEMENTS INVOLVED IN THE THREE TRAINING PROCESSES

How long does it take for a convert to become a disciple? a disciple a worker? a worker a leader? Because people are so different from one another, the time elements will vary. But general guidelines can be suggested. They are:

- Convert to disciple — 2 years
- Disciple to worker — 2 years
- Worker to leader — 3 years

These are just general figures, for with one person it may take less time and with another more. Possibly as you read these figures and think about them, you might feel that they represent too long a time. You might think that's too slow and that the processes can be followed in much less time.

With some unusually gifted and dedicated people, you might be able to take less time. But the Bible and my personal experience over the years have shown that the above figures are about what it takes me and others to accomplish the various objectives. Note how long it took Elijah to train Elisha and for Paul to train Timothy before these men were ready to go out on their own.

How long did Jesus actually spend with the men He trained, and how long would we need to spend with our men in light of the training processes of today? As a statistical "for instance," let's say Jesus spent twelve hours a day with His men for three years. That's 4,380 hours a year, and 13,140 hours in those three years.

If we were able to spend seven hours per week with a

person (four in church and three elsewhere)—and that's a high figure—it would mean that we would spend 365 hours a year with that man. At that rate it would take us *thirty -six years* to match the time frame used by Jesus. And He was the God-man; we're merely human flesh! Seven years is not too much to expect to do a quality work under the blessing and guidance of the Holy Spirit of God.

In addition, ask yourself these questions: Is your current program producing a band of faithful people who are able to teach others also? Is the method you have been using currently populating your church with a group of spiritually qualified workers? Would you rather have ten people established as disciples and equipped as workers, or one hundred people partially so? Your answers to these questions will determine your philosophy of the ministry of making disciples.

Also consider and meditate on these Scriptures: "He [a leader (an elder)] must not be a recent convert, or he may become conceited and fall under the same judgment as the devil" (1 Tim. 3:6). "They [leaders (deacons)] must first be tested; and then if there is nothing against them, let them serve as deacons" (1 Tim. 3:10). "Do not be hasty in the laying on of hands [on leadership], and do not share in the sins of others. Keep yourself pure" (1 Tim. 5:22).

Finally, consider the fact that when God grows an oak, He takes years; a toadstool can come up overnight! Faithful and skillful disciples, workers, and leaders take time to build.